JOHN MACMURRAY

Twentieth-Century Political Thinkers
Series Editors: Kenneth L. Deutsch and Jean Bethke Elshtain

JOHN MACMURRAY

Community beyond
Political Philosophy

FRANK G. KIRKPATRICK

ROWMAN & LITTLEFIELD PUBLISHERS, INC.
Lanham • Boulder • New York • Toronto • Oxford

ROWMAN & LITTLEFIELD PUBLISHERS, INC.

Published in the United States of America
by Rowman & Littlefield Publishers, Inc.
A wholly owned subsidary of The Rowman & Littlefield Publishing Group, Inc.
4501 Forbes Boulevard, Suite 200, Lanham, Maryland 20706
www.rowmanlittlefield.com

PO Box 317
Oxford
OX2 9RU, UK

British Library Cataloguing in Publication Information Available

Library of Congress Cataloging-in-Publication Data

Kirkpatrick, Frank G.
    John Macmurray : community beyond political philosophy / Frank G.
Kirkpatrick.
        p. cm. — (20th century political thinkers)
    Includes bibliographical references and index.
    ISBN 0-7425-2253-9 (hardcover : alk. paper) — ISBN 0-7425-2254-7 (pbk. :
alk. paper)
    1. Macmurray, John, 1891– I. Title. II. Series: Twentieth-century political
thinkers.

    B1647.M134K57 2005
    320'.092—dc22

                                                                    2004026155

Printed in the United States of America

♾™ The paper used in this publication meets the minimum requirements of
American National Standard for Information Sciences—Permanence of Paper for
Printed Library Materials, ANSI/NISO Z39.48-1992.

CONTENTS

1

INTRODUCTION

Will Kymlicka has asked the question that frames our understanding of the work of John Macmurray (1891–1976): "What more, or what else, is needed to sustain unity than shared political principles? This is one of the great unresolved questions of contemporary political philosophy."[1] John Macmurray's work does not fit easily into contemporary academic categories of classification. He devoted much thought to political philosophy but was not known primarily as a political philosopher. He wrote extensively on politics and political principles but never ran for political office. He understood the importance of the political sphere but never regarded it, or the state, as an end in itself. He was one of the most keenly informed scholars of Marx during his generation but was never a Marxist. He showed an initial interest in, even sympathy for, the principles of communism (always with serious qualifications) but became one of the Soviet Union's harshest critics.

He influenced a number of politicians, including Hugh Gaitskell, head of Britain's Labour Party, and more recently Prime Minister Tony Blair, but was never himself deeply involved in political activities beyond that of being instructor, advisor, and supporter to those who were. He was a philosopher who did not abandon metaphysics at a time when most other English philosophers were fleeing from it into the world of linguistic and logical analysis. He remained committed to philosophy's goal of understanding reality through a developed metaphysics while other philosophers were giving up on a universal discourse of meaning and settling for "incommensurate" language games.

He was a deeply religious thinker who did not abandon philosophy when the most influential theologians of his generation, such as Karl Barth, were seeking to transcend it. Although deeply religious, he was not a sectarian, nor a churchman in the traditional sense. He did not formally join a religious community until late in life, when he began an association with the Society of Friends, one of the least doctrinal or theologically rigid religious communities in the world.

He was a Christian but was not bound by many of the traditional doctrines of the Church. Much of his philosophy was centered on the work and teachings of Jesus, but he expressed no particular sympathy for creedal affirmations of Jesus' divinity. He was resolutely anti-dualist and anti-idealist while affirming what he took to be the core truths of Christianity (which had been taken by many of its followers to be decidedly dualist and idealist). His Christianity was profoundly rooted in what he understood to be a Hebraic mentality, by reference to which he judged the claims of the New Testament, especially about Jesus. He was informed in most of his work by the Bible but relatively uninformed by biblical scholarship.

He was deeply committed to the principles of scientific investigation while warning against turning genuine science into scientism and transgressing what he regarded as the boundaries of science. He was particularly insightful about the work of psychology (anticipating and to a small degree influencing contemporary object-relations theorists). Even as a philosopher committed to the use of reason, he was more sensitive than most to the role of emotions in human conduct.

For all his philosophical training and learning, he wrote in a deceptively simple, even naive way, often leading other philosophers to overlook the fundamental challenge of his work on epistemology and the role of religion in human life. He took on the thought of Descartes and Kant in carefully reasoned analysis but did not engage in footnote-laden, discursive, fine-grained analysis of the intricacies of their work.

He was a quintessential European, trained in the primary works of Western philosophy, religion, and culture. At the same time, he struggled to articulate truths about human beings that were universal and not simply the product of particular historical periods or cultures. He brought the realities of history to the fore in his thought (based as it was on the centrality of the self as agent who makes history), but he never surrendered to historicism. Very much part of the British culture, he tried to see beyond the limits of the English nation-state. Grounded in the principles of democracy, however, he never seriously believed that nondemocratic states could meet his standards of community, equity, and justice.

Above all, he was a political philosopher committed to putting politics into a wider, more comprehensive, metaphysical and religious framework.

Throughout his work he was trying, in effect, to answer Kymlicka's question: to provide the "something else" or "something more" beyond political principles that is needed to sustain human unity. He found that something more in what he called "community" (which he increasingly distinguished from the proper object of political philosophy—society) that is grounded in love, founded on God's intention for humankind, and developed by the fundamental human activity of religion. That something more than politics, quite simply, is the experience of persons living in community with each other. He believed that community (a concept I will define much more fully and precisely later) was the aspiration of all human beings. Community can be embedded in political societies and have a symbiotic relationship to them, but it is never reduced to or exhaustively identified with them. Unfortunately, given the profligate and multiple meanings that have been inscribed on the terms "community" and "persons in relation," even the term "love," Macmurray's insistence that political actions be understood in relation to the metaphysical primacy of persons in loving relations in community could easily be taken as naive, superficial, simplistic, and unsophisticated. I hope to show that none of these characteristics applies to his mature and developed thought.

But the key to understanding John Macmurray as political philosopher is to recognize that he grounds his political philosophy in a broader, deeper, metaphysical, even ontological philosophy that he called the "philosophy of the personal," at the heart of which is the notion that God created persons for mutual love in and through communities, for which, in part, human societies exist. And his understanding of community is itself grounded in a concept that makes religion the primary activity of human beings, to which political activity is ultimately subordinate.

NOTE

1. Will Kymlicka, *Contemporary Political Philosophy*, 2nd ed. (Oxford: Oxford University Press, 2002), 257.

2

AN INTELLECTUAL BIOGRAPHY
OF JOHN MACMURRAY: FROM
EVANGELICALISM TO MARXISM

The major appointments and events of John Macmurray's life are not the stuff of which romance or intrigue are made. He held major academic positions and was generally recognized during his lifetime as an important thinker, but he never achieved the eminence of many of his peers, including, for example, his successor as Grote Professor at University College, London, A. J. Ayer. He seems always to have remained in the shadow of more prominent colleagues, associates, and acquaintances such as Leonard Woolf, R. H. Tawney, A. D. Lindsay, and Karl Polanyi. Much of his nonacademic work was done with and for lay groups such as the listeners of the BBC, or the committed activists who made up the Christian Left in England in the 1930s, or with educational theorists.

Born in 1891 into a family steeped in Calvinist Scottish Presbyterianism, near Dumfries in the south of Scotland, John Macmurray was immersed in a religious environment in which, as his primary biographer John Costello has expressed it, "he was not to think of himself first or even to think of himself as of any particular value at all."[1] This injunction against self-love was not only rooted in the religion Macmurray imbibed from his parents, but it also became the foundation of his philosophy of the personal, in which the "other" was to be the primary object of one's love. His focus on the "other" was so intense that Macmurray called the orientation of love "heterocentric" in order to distinguish it from the "egocentric" orientation typical not only of a sinful attitude, but philosophically of a false epistemological starting point.

For a time Macmurray had considered missionary work, but he was also blessed with a particularly keen intellect, which he decided not to ignore. In 1909 he entered the University of Glasgow, where he embraced both the classics and science, winning a prize in 1912 for his work in geology.[2]

Having completed his degree in classics at Glasgow, Macmurray entered Balliol College, Oxford, in the fall of 1913 on a Snell Exhibition. At the time, Balliol was "grounded in liberal Christian conviction which linked human care for the world with the Gospel mandate to serve the Kingdom of God."[3] Macmurray would imbibe this spirit fully. His tutor was A. D. Lindsay, whose Christian socialist leanings, and in particular his commitment to democracy, would deeply influence Macmurray's later political philosophy.

When war was declared, Macmurray joined the ambulance corps of the British forces and soon found himself at the front. Costello recounts one episode during this period in which Macmurray claims to have seen a mysterious stranger who told him, as in a dream, "You will not be killed in this war. You will return to help remake the world."[4] He did eventually return from the war, but not without receiving a disfiguring scar on his face, which prompted him to grow a beard that he kept for the rest of his life.

One casualty of the war was Macmurray's latent utopianism about changing society in a Christian socialist direction. He writes in a letter: "my experience with men out here [the front] has undermined my faith in Socialism as a practical creed. . . . It seems to me that all these men . . . are quite incapable of passing judgment on any subject that is not entirely within the range of their own experience and training. Especially my attempts to get working men amongst them to subordinate their class idea to the idea of a state that includes it, has often been met by the statement that to do so seems honestly to them to be playing the traitor to their fellow workers. Doesn't that cut at the roots of all democratic government?"[5] Later his faith in socialism would revive as he encountered the work of Karl Marx and studied what he would call "the philosophy of communism."

A second effect of the war was his growing disenchantment with organized religion. Having spoken against the infatuation with war in a church on one of his brief returns from the front, he found himself shunned by the congregation. As he was later to recount, in what was the closest he came to an autobiography, he spoke to the parishioners about the insidious danger of continuing hatred toward the Germans: "I felt as though an evil spirit had entered them [his audience], a spirit of malice and hatred. Before twenty-four hours had passed I wanted to get back to the trenches, where for all the misery and destruction, the spiritual atmosphere was relatively clean. It was, I think, the ignorant and superstitious hatred of the Germans, and the equally ignorant and unreal glorification of us, in the trenches, as heroes that had this effect." Unfortunately, he recalled, "the congregation took it badly; I could feel a cold hostility menacing me; and no one spoke to me after the service was over."[6] Macmurray, in turn, made the decision to leave the churches behind while not abandoning in any way his commitment to the development of an authentic religious understanding of the world. His break with the churches was essentially based on his belief that they had become morally bankrupt, not that their theology was wrong.[7] Whatever within the Christianity he had inherited might fall to criticism, he remained convinced that "religion itself is not merely valid, but central in human life." Macmurray explained that "my personal development resulted in a deep skepticism of all the traditional expressions of religion, and so brought me down to the bedrock of a belief in the reality of religious experience; indeed in the validity of Christianity, whatever Christianity might really be. It left everything else doubtful."[8]

Refusing to separate religion from the core of what ought to constitute a healthy human society, he decided that he would dedicate his life, as a philosopher, to eliminating war. He brought to this task, he said later, "a mind that had become deeply skeptical of the principles underlying European civilization in which I had been brought up and which had issued in the savage destruction and stupid waste in which I had played a part."[9]

In the early summer of 1916 Macmurray received a commission as a second lieutenant in the Queen's Own Cameron Highlanders. After a brief visit home to get married, he returned to the front and, in March 1918, was severely wounded in the Battle of Arras. He received the Military Cross for bravery and leadership under fire, but for him the war was over. In early 1919 he returned to Oxford on a John Locke Scholarship. It was during this period that Macmurray gave up on the established churches, even as he was deepening his appreciation for religion. He was also becoming more committed to a life of professional philosophizing.

When he finished his degree work at Oxford, he accepted a position as lecturer in philosophy under Samuel Alexander at Manchester University.[10] He remained in that position for only sixteen months, moving in 1921 to a chair of philosophy at the University of Witwatersrand in Johannesburg, South Africa. Macmurray read and commented critically on Bernard Bosanquet's *Philosophical Theory of the State* and was particularly taken by the biological imagery of organism around which much of political philosophy under the influence of Hegel was being structured. This organic model runs the risk, as he would later argue at greater length, of subordinating the individual to the totality of the organism as a whole, that is, to the state. He found in medieval philosophy a necessary counter-balance to this motif of subordination: "political thought, when it is genuinely Mediaeval, starts from the Whole but ascribes an intrinsic value to every partial whole down to and including the Individual."[11] His critique of the organic model would become the basis for his later attack on fascism and even on Marxism (though he was initially drawn to the latter for its humanistic aspects). This theme of the individual's relation to the state would become the basis for much of Macmurray's later development of a distinctive political philosophy, built upon his "philosophy of the personal" in which *community* is set in dialectical tension with *society*.

In 1922 Macmurray received a call to become a fellow and tutor at his old college, Balliol. He was also appointed Jowett Lecturer in Philosophy, replacing his old tutor, A. D. Lindsay (who had moved to the chair in moral philosophy at Glasgow). Among his students in those years were Dorothy Emmett, John Findlay (who became a major Hegelian scholar), Hugh Gaitskell (later a political philosopher at University College, London, and subsequently head of the Labour Party), and Sir Richard Acland, also a strong supporter of Labour and a cofounder of the Commonwealth Movement in the 1940s, which had a brief moment in the political sun before disappearing.[12]

It is from this period that Macmurray's earliest scholarly work emanated. He read widely in the history of Western philosophy, particularly theories of government. Many of his early publications began to deal with the nature of human society, its form of government, and its relation to what he took to be Christian insights into human fellowship. From the beginning of his philosophical career, the nature of human society and the conditions that make it possible and preservative of the fullness of human personality are at the center of Macmurray's work. In an early piece titled "Christianity— Pagan or Scientific?" in the *Hibbert Journal*, he sounded the first notes of his later political philosophy, seeking to find the basis for a universal human fellowship.[13] He contrasts Plato's vision of an exclusive republic of like-minded persons with what he takes to be Christ's vision of a society that he described as a "universal family." This vision constituted a "unity of purpose," which Macmurray understood to be the final realization of a universal unity achievable through love, not coercion, fear, or exclusion.

In the process of sketching this view, Macmurray made a clean break with the doctrinal certainties of the religion of his childhood. He now insisted that true Christianity is "scientific" in the sense that it denies certainty and works by experiment and the testing of hypotheses regarding the development of human society. He became firmly committed to the notion that "all philosophy has practical implications. A theory of metaphysics implies a theory of social activity. The facts of human history are therefore the most eloquent of all criticisms upon philosophical systems."[14] This view, which he steadfastly refused to call "pragmatic," is nonetheless remarkably close to the American school of thought developed by William James, Charles Sanders Peirce, and John Dewey, who most closely resembled Macmurray. In his fully developed philosophy of action, Macmurray developed a form of epistemological pragmatism but seemed to show no familiarity with the work of the American pragmatists, despite his essential agreement on the need to test all ideas by practice and his agreement, in principle, with Dewey's attack on the quest for certainty.

He also began to write regular pieces for *British Weekly*. One of his earliest submissions critiqued the Hegelian-influenced organic philosophy of the state found in J. C. Smut's *Holism and Evolution* because it ignored the reflexive character of personal consciousness.[15] At about the same time, Macmurray also contributed many short articles to the *Auxiliary Movement*,[16] associated with the *Student Movement*. One of the first pieces he wrote for this informal journal, "Economic Laws and Social Progress," argues against the certainty of so-called economic "laws," which are, like all laws of science, generalizations subject to change as time and conditions change. This view becomes part of a lifelong belief on his part that all human action is subject to revision in the light of human purposes as they are enacted in history. Economic laws, in particular, are generalizations that are "exceedingly likely to break down in practice for one reason or another."[17] Macmurray was trying to place economic practices and the science that studies them into a larger value-based and societal context. "Economic life depends partly (not wholly) and essentially upon human desires, human valuations and human ideals."[18] Economic change, therefore, requires a change in human nature, one that reaches below the surface and into "the unconscious tendencies and the ingrained habits of the race."[19]

Macmurray was already struggling with the issue of how conscious, purposeful human action can reshape the economic conditions in which people either are stultified or assisted in their intentions to live more meaningful lives. For him this can only happen in a more equitable society, one that, as he would argue in his more mature philosophy, supports the experience of mutual love, fellowship, and personal community.

This struggle increasingly involved Macmurray in a critical analysis of organic models of society in which the individual is valued more for functionality than for individuality as a person. In his first explicitly political philosophical article, "Government by the People," Macmurray opposed the notion that the state should control the moral and cultural activities of life.[20]

In arguing that government must respect the rights of minorities and conscientious objectors, Macmurray, aligning himself explicitly with the Christian insistence on the autonomy of the individual in all matters of conscience, says that "freedom of conscience, freedom of association, freedom of individual initiative, freedom for any man who wills to plan creatively and accomplish his purposes, freedom for small minorities from the tyranny, not only of government officials, but of public opinion, these are the things for which democracy has striven and is still striving. We have aimed . . . to prevent the complex of organic institutions . . . from throttling the liberty and power of individual human beings to live spontaneously up to the limits of their capacity."[21] Morality and what he calls the "spiritual outlook" must be freed from control by the state. They are the province of religion, whose essence it is "to control the whole life of culture and conscience, to unify and to inspire it."[22] This claim is based on his assumption that "behind the democratic movement lies the Christian insistence upon the supreme and final value of individual personality."[23]

At the same time, he claimed that the spiritual outlook was becoming more international and universal. This anticipates Macmurray's development of the notion of a universal community in which the nation-state has, at best, a provisional, pragmatic utility. Nevertheless, he argued, the state has an important if limited and subordinate role to play in the life of persons living together—the role of the state is to provide the material support for such a life. And one crucial ingredient in complex societies of "organic social network(s)" is the development and maintenance of law and justice. "The basis of the state is the categorical imperative of justice. Yet even in the moral life justice is no all-inclusive obligation, but merely its basis and its beginning."[24] Political obligation is derivative from a more basic moral obligation.

Clearly, in these sentiments Macmurray was trying to find what Kymlicka called that something more than shared political principles that is needed to sustain unity, something that goes beyond political analysis, philosophy, and practice in providing the ultimate meaning of people living together. Macmurray called this something more "religion" or the "spiritual outlook" but hardly defined what he meant by it except that it has something to do with individual personality and morality. At the heart of his political philosophy is the preservation of personality, which he believes is endangered by Hegelianism and its organic categories, in which the self is swallowed up as a moment in a more basic, more real, organic whole.[25] As Macmurray developed this notion of personality, it would become more defined by its relation to other persons in bonds of fellowship and mutual love, rather than in strictly political relations, which become subordinate and functional to fellowship. This would be the basis for his later, more carefully worked-out distinction between society (law and justice) and community (love and fellowship).

By 1929 Macmurray was pushing forward with his belief that religious convictions must not be the basis for the actions of the state. In a piece in the *British Weekly* in late 1929, he argued that states have the right to determine their own internal affairs, but not an unlimited right. If a nation "indulges in organized massacre of minorities," other nations have a moral obligation to interfere. At the same time, the nations of the world ought to be seeking to extend the influence of "international law."[26] While Macmurray wanted the state out of the business of determining the moral convictions of its citizens, he was also assuming a comprehensive, even universal moral framework within which to put his evaluation of the utility of the state. The defense of the moral framework would come only when he had fully worked out the relation between religion (whose intention is the full development of the individual personality), community (the only social locus within which that development is possible), and society (the material and legal support for both the individual and the community).

The first attempt to work out this moral framework came in an article in the *Journal of Philosophical Studies* in 1929. In "The Unity of Modern Problems," he first sketched the tripartite schema of models of understanding the world.[27] He calls these models the mechanical, the organic, and the personal. They are applied to what he calls the fundamental problem of modern thinking, "the attempt to understand the nature of the self and its self-realization."[28] The first model for understanding the self is to conceive of it as a substance, a unit embedded in a field of causal law. Under this model, the self is understood mathematically and mechanically, as a thing identical in substance to all other things. In this view, the state is a complex of identical units with no intrinsic differences, arranged according to their social positions. There must be no appeal to the individual qualities that distinguish one person from another. Each unit is determined solely by external forces, and thus the whole schema falls under strict causal law as articulated by science. No actions are self-determined, and this flies in the face of our intuitive sense of ourselves as, at least in part, self-determining agents.[29]

The second model conceives of the self as an organism embedded in an even more complex organism. This model starts from the fact that some things are clearly alive and evidence growth, while other things do not. But growth, in the organic model, is not directed by the intentions of a personal agent. As Macmurray said in the fuller treatment of this idea four years later:

"the teleological description of the process of growth is not offered as an explanation of why the growth takes place, but merely as a description of the fact. In no sense does organic teleology imply purpose or even purposiveness."[30]

Differences between the elements of the organism are recognized, but only as functional to the whole of which they are a part. Macmurray found this view unacceptable because it fails to express the true nature of selfhood or to "form the basis of a conscious construction of human relations, of a deliberate self-expression, which lies at the basis of all the problems of the present day."[31] In short, it destroys the individuality of the selves that constitute the organism.[32] "The organic formula deprives the individual elements of their uniqueness. They are essentially complementary, each relative to the others. Only in functional connection with the other elements has each any being in the whole. Thus the whole value of each element depends upon its subordination . . . to the whole complex; none of the organs of the body have any value except in so far as they subserve the function of the whole." He acknowledged that this organic view had led to some of the most important political changes of the past century. If every organ is necessary to the successful functioning of the whole, then each organ has some structural value. On this basis the abolition of slavery was built, and in the more recent past (he clearly had Marx in mind here), it led to legislation for the protection of the poor, the worker, and so forth.[33]

Yet the organism as a whole is functionless. It has no environment in which its function is determined. "We are swallowed up in an endless and meaningless relativity. We ask, 'What is it all for?' and we are told 'For the good of the community.' But this means nothing, unless there is a 'good' of the community which is something other than the baker's baking or the spinner's spinning, or even the member of Parliament's speechifying, and the philosopher's droning."[34] This organic model is exemplified in Rousseau's "general will," which is an organic will, a blind will, a name for the organic impulse to keep feeding the organism (which has no external purpose but its own survival).

The failure of this model to preserve the intrinsic value of the self requires us, Macmurray argued, to move to a third mode of understanding the self, which he calls the personal. The authentic person is an organism but not *only* an organism. Personality is something higher than organic life, "something that subordinates to itself and uses for its purposes the structures and functional harmonies that life, in its passage, builds up and maintains." We need the complex organic political institutions that work for the "satisfaction of our humanity." But there are multiple such organic institutions.

None of them alone can fulfill the individual personality. "The Self turns out to be super-organic. It cannot express itself through an organic structure—not in its essential unity."[35] Macmurray concluded this vitally important transitional essay by proclaiming that "the unity of modern problems is the problem of discovering or constructing . . . a new schema of the Self . . . which will enable us to construct . . . a civilization whose mechanical and organic structures will be at the service of a personal life, whose meaning and essence is friendship."[36]

Only other persons can bring out in us our full personhood. "Only in a full personal relationship with another person do I find a response at my own level . . . so that for the first time I can achieve self-consciousness. . . . I am because I know you, and . . . you are because you know me."[37] In the personal mode of relationship, the persons in relation "do not lose their individuality to become functional elements in an individuality which includes them both. . . . In the personal field the only real individuals are individual persons. Groups of persons are not individuals."[38]

The political implications of this understanding are never far from Macmurray's thought. He concluded *Interpreting the Universe* by arguing that the organic model of persons is essential to the functional organization of society, which itself is necessary for providing the economic conditions "without which it is not possible to release man from bondage to his environment and to enable him to dominate and utilize it." And the ultimate justification of dominating and utilizing the environment is "the achievement of a community of persons, as persons, to which it is the means."[39] In a sentence that anticipates the thrust of most of his political thought during the decade of the 1930s, he adds that the "problem of subordinating the social control of life through economic organization to the human interests of all the individuals concerned is quite obviously the emergent social problem of the contemporary world."[40] His task will be to interpret the political philosophies of Marx, socialism, and communism in light of their utility in bringing about the social, material, and economic conditions that make for (but do not constitute or exhaust) the fullness of human life lived in communities of persons as persons. He will build a philosophy of society as a prerequisite for a philosophy of community.

MACMURRAY IN THE 1930s

The 1930s was the decade of Macmurray's greatest output of work on political philosophy, especially in his engagement with the thought of Karl

Marx. His first academic piece published in the decade was "The Conception of Society," a talk he gave to the Aristotelian Society in March 1931. Although he used the word "society" in a way that suggests he really intended to describe "community," the article lays down some of the markers for what he takes to be the ideal form of social life.

He was clearly trying to edge beyond traditional political philosophy, which focuses on the nature of the political entity and not necessarily on the moral or spiritual foundations on which it rests, or on the extra-political quality of the relationships among its members. It is a truism, he conceded, that human beings are inherently social. One view of this sociality holds that society is itself an entity of which we are all members and which must be treated as having rights of its own that can be asserted against the individuals who comprise it. The other view of sociality, which he calls "adjectival," sees society as a quality of human life that is broader and deeper than the social forms it takes. It is "the mutuality of human life,"[41] a phrase that he repeats with variations in all his later work on community.

If we think of society only as an entity in itself, it is easy to confuse it with the state. The result of this confusion is to identify membership in the society with citizenship in a nation-state "and so to provide a limit of political organization to the nexus of social relationships." In the adjectival conception of society, on the other hand, the sharing of human experience, the experience of other persons as persons, is central.[42] In society individuals become aware that they share experience with others, that they are not alone. They discover that in a sense they are constituted by their relationships with others.[43] "The realization of society involves the achievement of a real mutuality of shared experience."[44]

A subtheme in his argument is that objectivity is a crucial component of our understanding of others. This argument was vitally important for his full development of what it means to stand in relationship to other persons. It is possible that in choosing the word "objectivity," Macmurray was deliberately trying to counter the increasing emphasis by theologians of his time on existential subjectivity. An emphasis on subjectivity threatens to undermine the genuine "otherness" of other persons (i.e., their objectivity to the subject) and undercuts the possibility of authentic human relationships between distinct and individual persons. By objectivity Macmurray means "the capacity to transcend the limits of the self and to live, in thought, by the nature of that which is not the self; to think [and act] in terms of a nature which lies beyond the limits of our own nature."[45] He means to live, think, and act in relation to others in their own terms. If I do not recognize that some other persons possess the same capabilities as myself, I will not experience what only other persons can do: namely to elicit from me my capacity for love, mutuality, reciprocity, compassion, trust, and so forth. To bring this subtheme back to the issue of society, Macmurray argued that human society is not just the *fact* of human relationships but, more importantly, "the consciousness of these relationships as a factor in the consciousness of the individuals so related."[46]

These reflections suggest that Macmurray was already struggling to articulate a conception of human togetherness that goes beyond mere political association into a more substantive form of relationship. The question this leads to, of course, is what are the social/economic conditions that a society must have if the fullness of the human capacity for shared mutual experience is to be realized? That is the question that drove Macmurray into his early interest in the work of Marx and communism as a philosophy.

At virtually the same time that he was developing these ideas in print, Macmurray was given the opportunity to express them over the airwaves as well. Possibly at the suggestion of Archbishop William Temple, his name was given to the BBC for a series of radio talks beginning in the spring and summer of 1930 and continuing through January 1932.[47] These talks formed the basis for his first book, *Freedom in the Modern World*, published in 1932. It was followed a few years later by *Reason and Emotion*,[48] also based on radio talks. Macmurray explicitly based these talks on a quasi-Marxian assumption that "philosophy becomes real . . . only when its problems are forced upon it by the immediate life of its time and its environment."[49] In his opinion, the crisis that lies behind what he calls the "modern dilemma" is clearly economic.[50] But, he argued, pushing beyond the limits of understanding society exclusively in economic and political terms, "we will never solve our economic troubles till we have solved the dilemma in our spiritual life which produces them."[51] Here again we glimpse the "something more" that Macmurray is trying to articulate to take his philosophy beyond political philosophy in its narrower forms.

At the heart of these talks and books is a fuller development of the need persons have to live in terms of the objective reality of others. This reality must engage not just our intellects but our feelings as well. Without feelings there can be no genuine choices made as to how to relate to others (both human and nonhuman). Intellect can help to inform our action, but it cannot by itself give us the intention or value, or what Macmurray calls "faith," by which we will be moved to act. That can come only from the emotional dimension of our being. And the one human activity that seeks, in principle, to unify both the intellectual and emotional dimensions within us is religion. Religion arises out of our emotional life as a "response of the whole of our personality to the whole of life" and includes both reason and emotion[52] unified so as to help us live a more fulfilling life, especially in our relations with other feeling/thinking beings, namely, other persons.

The problem, as Macmurray stated it, is that we have allowed our emotions (which always underlie our choices) to remain uneducated and undeveloped.[53] We have highly developed intellects and the economic, military, and political tools that reflect rationality, but we have allowed our more primitive emotions to control the use of them.

Macmurray claimed that there are two basic emotional attitudes: love and fear. Love, he argued, is the primary emotion and draws us toward other persons. Fear is a secondary emotion that emerges when our love is frustrated or betrayed. In fear, we seek to withdraw from relationships with others because we fear being hurt. Love connects us with others; fear isolates us and turns us into *individualists* (not to be confused with *individuals*, which we all are, in distinct and particular ways). In fear, we regard the world as hostile, and we seek security and protection from it.[54] But the great mistake we make when we live by fear is to ignore the fact that fear keeps us from being who we really are. It ultimately frustrates us in the full development of our personhood. "When we concentrate on defending ourselves against the world outside us, against nature and other nations and other people, we are frustrating ourselves; and the more successful we are in achieving security, the more completely do we frustrate ourselves. For what are we afraid of? What are we defending ourselves against? Against life—against our own life, the life that is us."[55] To be truly free persons, we must come to grips with what is real. Ideas or emotions that do not correspond in some deep sense to the world as it really is will keep us the prisoners of a fear-filled, unfulfilled life.

We can, of course, be mistaken in what we take to be real, as we discover when we try to act on a false belief or false emotion. Unreal things ultimately let us down. Macmurray argued that the test of the reality of an idea or feeling is in action. "Things are only discovered to be unreal *in use*. The only test of unreality is a practical test. . . . False beliefs break down in practice in the long run. And that is as true of false ideals and false moralities, of false government and false religion."[56]

The relation between our thought patterns and the objective world is also the theme of Macmurray's *Interpreting the Universe*, from which we took his understanding of the organic form of relationship a little earlier. His fundamental claim was that the primary experience of persons is being in active relationship with what is other than themselves. In what he calls "immediate experience," we know at a nontheoretical level what we are doing. When our intentions are frustrated or impeded in our activity, we step back from that experience and try to figure out what has gone awry. Reflection presupposes prior activity, which has not, up to that point, been thought about. Action precedes thought. This will form the basis for his radical critique of Western epistemology in the Gifford Lectures of the early 1950s. "If there were no such thing as action, there could be no discussion of it. There would be nothing to discuss. If there were no immediate experience there could be no reflection, because there would be nothing to reflect upon."[57] The nature of this immediate experience is unity and completeness. "Nothing in it is really separate from anything else. . . . It is unified with and coextensive with feeling and action. It is our consciousness in living rather than our consciousness of living. In immediate experience we know anything by being interested in it, by desiring it, by loving or hating it, and above all, by doing things with it . . . cognition, conation and feeling—are fused into a single whole in the living experience."[58]

When we reflect on this unity, after it has been broken by something going wrong, we stop acting in the immediate sense and perform a kind of derivative action: the action of thinking. But our thought is instrumental to the successful resumption of primary action, the return to the unity and completeness of immediate experience. And reality is "bound up with the unity and completeness of the world in our immediate experience of it."[59]

If the fullest, most satisfying kind of experience is one in which we relish the fullness of our own personal reality, then we need to use our intellectual knowledge to figure out what kind of reality will make that possible. Macmurray believed that at the heart of our personal reality is "spontaneous objectivity" and that "it is our nature to apprehend and enjoy a world that is outside ourselves, to live in communion with a world which is independent of us. . . . And when we are completely ourselves we live by that knowledge and appreciation of what is not ourselves, and so in communion with other beings. That is what I term our objectivity, and it is the essence of our human nature."[60]

Both in his time and ours, this is a radical claim. Its trajectory is the opposite of that which existentialism (quite popular in Macmurray's time) proposed. It takes us out of ourselves, not more deeply into ourselves. It does so because the fullness of human life consists in relationships with beings who are genuinely "other," that is, who have unique, individualizing, particular characteristics that distinguish individual ones of them as *this* being, or *that* being, not just as a being-in-general. And yet, it is only in appreciating this otherness that we come back to ourselves as the relational beings we fundamentally are. There are clearly echoes here of Hegel's notion of the going-out and coming-back of God, but they are echoes only. Macmurray did not elaborate on their tonality, keeping them strictly within the boundaries of relationality, not aspiring to Hegel's ideal of the Absolute as being-at-home-with-self, self-sufficient, united with itself.[61] In Hegel, relationality is the penultimate stage prior to total freedom that is to have no "other" standing alongside oneself. In Macmurray, relationality is the ultimate stage of fullness and requires the "other" to stand alongside one as the unique other with and through whom one's relational capacity is fulfilled.

But what particular other beings bring us to the fullness of experience? What beings allow us to be most fully ourselves? The answer, which is at the heart of his entire philosophy of community, is simply other persons enjoyed in human friendship. "Human nature expresses itself most concretely and completely in friendship."[62]

The world is filled, of course, with multiple and diverse kinds of beings. The epistemological question is how does one best characterize the world that is most adequate to the development of friendship, communion, mutuality, and being most completely ourselves? The answer, for Macmurray, was the personal unity pattern, which he initially sketched out in *Interpreting the Universe* and then developed fully in the Gifford Lectures.

Two essential components in understanding the personal unity pattern are conceptual accuracy and emotional reality, or objectivity. Feeling is the basis for grasping the value of things external to us. It is the ground of relationality. We can, of course, misvalue things: we can have emotional attitudes toward others that are unreal, that mislead us in relations with them. We may feel fear in the presence of something that we take to be an angry bear while all the time it is a cardboard poster picturing a bear. Our fear is misplaced or misdirected.

Love is one of those emotions that directs us out of ourselves and toward others. But we can mistake mere infatuation or erotic desire for genuine love. Or we can suppress the love we feel for another and deny that we feel it. More seriously, we can fall in love with love itself, rather than with the other person. Feelings that have as their object simply themselves are what Macmurray called "unreal" or sentimental because they do not connect us with the reality outside ourselves.[63]

Since love is the central emotion of relationality between persons, it is important to understand how Macmurray understood it. Love, he said, is *of* the other person. "Real love grasps the worth and value of its object and loves the other person for himself or herself. Unreal or sentimental love does not. It enjoys the feelings which the other person arouses or stimulates, and is not concerned with the real worth, the real goodness of its object."[64]

Why am I introducing this excursus into love and relationality at this point in Macmurray's intellectual development, since it will be more fully developed later? Why introduce it just as he is about to engage in a deep analysis of Marxian thought? The answer is that Marx will give him an understanding (which Macmurray will decide is ultimately flawed and insufficient) of the "real" conditions of the world toward which we had better have the right feelings and about which our thinking ought to be correct. Part of what it means to be fully human is to be able to exercise our capacity for freedom with as few unreal restraints as possible. And true freedom, Macmurray believed, is our ability to live fully in terms of the nature we have been given by God. "To be free . . . is to express one's own nature in action."[65] But if I am myself fully only when I am in relation to other real persons, then they must be free as well. This means that the material and social conditions of human life must be conducive to reality and to the freedom of others that is a prerequisite for our own freedom. This requires, in particular, conditions that do not turn persons into mere instruments for the successful political functioning of the organic society. The danger of Marxist organicism is reducing persons to their political functions and denying them their reality as full persons. If you tell a person "that he ought to serve society, work for the betterment of conditions in the future, identify himself with the cause of progress . . . then you are denying him his right to be a person, to be himself, to be real."[66] Macmurray's critique of politics and economic conditions presupposes that they are instrumental to a greater and more important end, namely, the fulfillment of persons in and through personal relationships.

One political implication Macmurray drew from this analysis was that we must get over a sentimental treatment of the poor. We must move beyond "vague benevolence for people in general."[67] What the poor need is not pity from a distance "but their bare rights as members of an astonishingly wealthy community."[68] At the same time, we need to avoid handing social problems over to state organizations that, for the most part, have made life poorer, not richer. Too much reliance on the state teaches people to put their faith in politics, which in Macmurray's day meant either bolshevism or fascism, both of which rest on "the deification of organized society."[69] Both reduce the full reality of the person to its place in the social organization, rather than seeing social organization as an instrument for the material and political conditions that form the basis for (but do not contain the essence of) the full development of human personality in mutual love and friendship. Macmurray confessed he didn't want either bolshevism or fascism but if forced to choose would pick bolshevism "because at least it repudiates the belief in mere wealth."[70]

In two separate pieces of political analysis in 1933, Macmurray went further in his preliminary and sketchy treatment of fascism and what he now called communism (not bolshevism). In "Fascism?" written for the magazine *New Britain*, Macmurray identified himself as the president of the New Britain Initiative, an explicitly anti-fascist group. In the article, Macmurray distinguished between nationality and nationalism. The latter is a political policy that exploits the natural sentiments of nationality. Fascism is the most fanatical and irrational form of nationalism that uses "some of the noblest of human sentiments for the cheapest and nastiest of human purposes. . . . It is an effort to bamboozle the sincere, plain loyalty of simple people into supporting the lust of the few for power and prestige."[71]

A few years earlier, in a private letter, Macmurray railed against both nationalism and the "the worship of the state and organization." He had been trying in his BBC lectures to persuade his listeners that "nationality is not an ideal but a historical accident—a combination of political unity with cultural unity. And the democratic ideal is to thrust the state right out of the cultural field and keep it out. . . . It seems to me no reason for any particular state organization except a utilitarian one. Political unity is a means to an end, and the best state is the state that works best; which means, I think, the one that secures the maximum of justice. . . . Above all, we mustn't think of the state as if it were a cultural or a moral entity. I even go to the length of saying that the state ought never, on any account, to base its actions on moral grounds."[72]

This extraordinary statement begins to make sense when we remember that Macmurray had already started to sketch out a political philosophy in which the state is the instrument of justice, but the values on which it rests must be provided to it, as it were, from the outside, from religious sources. As he understood religion, it is clearly nonconfessional and nonsectarian.[73] Religion is concerned with the development of universal community, with the reconciliation of persons with each other and with the world in which they are intentional agents. This development requires the establishment of instruments and organizations as provisional aids, but they are not the central purpose of human life, which ought to be enjoyment of mutuality in relationship—that is, of friendship.

The week after "Fascism?" appeared, Macmurray published in the same magazine a second piece, "What About Communism?" It's the first published piece in which he took up the case of communism and began his nearly decade-long exploration of communism and Marxian thought.[74] At the same time, his book *The Philosophy of Communism* was being published. In the article on communism, Macmurray announced an attitude of "critical sympathy."[75] He claimed that, at least in intention if not in practice, communism is for the "realization in the economic field of freedom and equality" and is therefore "in the apostolic succession of the democratic movement . . . [which] lies in the control of the persons who hold power by the masses of people whose lives are affected for good or evil by the use that is made of that power."[76] In particular, this means that "the ownership of the means of production must pass to the community." The critical part of critical sympathy, however, lies in Macmurray's belief that the power of the state ought never to be used to force a new social order upon the people, because freedom, which is essential to a healthy society, cannot be coerced. Such coercion would eventually drive communism toward fascism. If what he called British socialism was to be created, it must be through voluntary initiative and a "voluntary acceptance of social discipline, in a thousand diverse ways, groups which have achieved in themselves a new community of co-operation."[77]

Like the communists, Macmurray did not think capitalism and democracy could co-exist.[78] Democracy requires the right to criticize and participate in the formation of economic and social policies. Each citizen must have the same right to such participation, and this is what Macmurray means by equality. But social/political/economic equality does not mean the eradication of individual differences: "difference is not the same thing as inequality. . . . It is because of these differences and in order to enrich human life by the full and free self-development of these differences that we must insist on equality. To be equal is not to be the same. It is to have recognized and provided for the right of every man to be himself in the expression of his inherent difference from others."[79]

Ultimately, neither fascism nor communism is acceptable because full human self-realization means "thinking and feeling really, for ourselves, and expressing our own reality in word and action. And this is freedom, and the secret of it lies in our capacity for friendship."[80] Friendship is best prepared for and its conditions provided for by a particular political/economic organization of society, but the content of friendship is unique to personal relations, and no structure of the state can substitute for it.

NOTES.

1. John Costello, *John Macmurray: A Biography* (Edinburgh: Floris Books, 2002), 26. Costello's book, to which I am profoundly indebted for its wealth of detail on

Macmurray's life, is the first full-scale biography of Macmurray and the first to draw not only on his published lectures and class notes but also on unpublished diaries, correspondence, and interviews with his family and friends.

2. Costello, *John Macmurray*, 47.

3. Costello, *John Macmurray*, 58.

4. Costello, *John Macmurray*, 68.

5. Quoted in Costello, *John Macmurray*, 74.

6. John Macmurray, *Search for Reality in Religion*, Swarthmore Lecture, 1965 (London: Allen and Unwin, 1965), 20–21.

7. Costello, *John Macmurray*, 89.

8. Macmurray, *Search for Reality in Religion*, 23.

9. Macmurray, *Search for Reality in Religion*, 22.

10. Costello, *John Macmurray*, 91.

11. Costello, *John Macmurray*, 102.

12.   Costello, *John Macmurray*, 120.

13. John Macmurray, "Christianity—Pagan or Scientific?" *Hibbert Journal* 24 (1925–26): 421–33. At this stage of his thinking, the terms "society" and "community" are used virtually interchangeably, though later he will make a clear, but complementary, distinction between them.

14. John Macmurray, "The Function of Experiment in Knowledge," *Proceedings of the Aristotelian Society* 27 (1926–1927): 212.

15. John Macmurray, "General Smuts as Philosopher," *British Weekly*, January 20, 1927, 418.

16. Self-described as a "comradeship of men and women who desire to understand the Christian faith, to find the Christian way, and to live the Christian life." See the following citation.

17. John Macmurray, "Economic Laws and Social Progress," *Auxiliary Movement* 29 (February 1927): 117.

18. Macmurray, "Economic Laws and Social Progress," 141.

19. Macmurray, "Economic Laws and Social Progress," 142.

20. John Macmurray, "Government by the People," *Journal of Philosophical Studies* 2 (1927): 532–43.

21. Macmurray, "Government by the People," 538–39.

22. Macmurray, "Government by the People," 542.

23. Macmurray, "Government by the People," 542.

24. Macmurray, "Government by the People," 543.

25. See John Macmurray, "The Principle of Personality in Experience," *Proceedings of the Aristotelian Society* 29 (1928–1929): 316, in which he says "any philosophy which I can accept must find Hegelianism, in its treatment of personality and of history, 'wholly alien.'"

26. John Macmurray, "The Limits of Interference Between Sovereign States," *British Weekly*, December 26, 1929, 284.

27. They would be developed more fully in his first book, *Interpreting the Universe*, published in 1933.

28. John Macmurray, "The Unity of Modern Problems," *Journal of Philosophical Studies* 4 (1929): 164.

29. See John Macmurray, *Interpreting the Universe* (London: Faber and Faber, 1933), 100–102.

30. Macmurray, *Interpreting the Universe*, 114.

31. Macmurray, "The Unity of Modern Problems," 171.

32. It is quite clear that he has in mind Hegel and possibly Whitehead when he writes of the organic view.

33. Macmurray, "The Unity of Modern Problems," 173.

34. Macmurray, "The Unity of Modern Problems," 175.

35. Macmurray, "The Unity of Modern Problems," 176–77.

36. Macmurray, "The Unity of Modern Problems," 179.

37. Macmurray, *Interpreting the Universe*, 136–37.

38. Macmurray, *Interpreting the Universe*, 140.

39. Macmurray, *Interpreting the Universe*, 153.

40. Macmurray, *Interpreting the Universe*, 153.

41. John Macmurray, "The Conception of Society," *Proceedings of the Aristotelian Society* 31 (1930 1931): 129.

42. Macmurray, "The Conception of Society," 135.

43. This notion of the self as constituted by its relation with others will only be fully developed some twenty years later in his 1953–1954 Gifford Lectures, *The Self as Agent*, and especially *Persons in Relation*.

44. Macmurray, "The Conception of Society," 138.

45. Macmurray, "The Conception of Society," 136–37.

46. Macmurray, "The Conception of Society," 138. Later he will substitute the term "intention" for the term "consciousness."

47. Macmurray admits that these talks were regarded by some people as "revolutionary and even disruptive." John Macmurray, *Freedom in the Modern World* (London: Faber and Faber, 1932), 8.

48. John Macmurray, *Reason and Emotion* (New York: Barnes and Noble, 1962), originally published in the United Kingdom in 1935.

49. Macmurray, *Freedom in the Modern World*, 11. He does not explicitly identify this view with Marx, but as we shall see, he is beginning his exploration of Marx at just this time and so it may be more than coincidental that he puts his premise in this form.

50. "The crisis which we are facing (or refusing to face) [is] in our economic and industrial activities." Macmurray, *Freedom in the Modern World*, 18.

51. Macmurray, *Freedom in the Modern World*, 18.

52. Macmurray, *Freedom in the Modern World*, 53.

53. Macmurray, *Freedom in the Modern World*, 51. "Action is necessarily determined by feeling. We cannot follow our intellects unless our feelings will allow this."

And as he says in *Reason and Emotion*, "our emotional life is *us* in a way our intellectual life cannot be; in that it alone contains the motives from which our conduct springs," 49.

54. Macmurray, *Freedom in the Modern World*, 55.

55. Macmurray, *Freedom in the Modern World*, 56.

56. Macmurray, *Freedom in the Modern World*, 127.

57. Macmurray, *Interpreting the Universe*, 13.

58. Macmurray, *Interpreting the Universe*, 22.

59. Macmurray, *Interpreting the Universe*, 34.

60. Macmurray, *Freedom in the Modern World*, 178.

61. G. W. F. Hegel, *On Art, Religion, Philosophy*, ed. J. Glenn Gray (New York: Harper and Row, 1970), 230, taken from the introduction to *Hegel's Lectures on the History of Philosophy*.

62. Macmurray, *Freedom in the Modern World*, 179.

63. Macmurray, *Freedom in the Modern World*, 148.

64. Macmurray, *Freedom in the Modern World*, 149.

65. Macmurray, *Freedom in the Modern World*, 166.

66. Macmurray, *Freedom in the Modern World*, 195.

67. Macmurray, *Freedom in the Modern World*, 211.

68. Macmurray, *Freedom in the Modern World*, 211.

69. Macmurray, *Freedom in the Modern World*, 213.

70. Macmurray, *Freedom in the Modern World*, 213.

71. John Macmurray, "Fascism?" *New Britain*, June 7, 1933, 70.

72. Letter to Donald Grant, June 5, 1930, quoted in Costello, *John Macmurray*, 190–91.

74. In another personal letter, Macmurray expresses his increasing alienation from "official" Christianity. To his friend Richard Roberts, he muses that he is a "bit obsessed now with the fear that I am sheltering under the wing of a Christianity that I don't really believe in. . . . I feel inclined to write a pamphlet on the question 'Was Christ a Christian?' with a thoroughly negative answer. What Christianity there is seems to me sometimes so completely bound up with a civilization that is, in my opinion, pretty fundamentally incompatible with the attitude of Christ." Quoted in Costello, *John Macmurray*, 166. The letter comes at the end of a 1929 conference to which he was invited to give the keynote address by William Temple (then archbishop of York, later archbishop of Canterbury) on the theme "The Purpose of God in the Life of the World." A. D. Lindsay, among others, was present. In his address, Macmurray argues for the necessary relationship between friendship and freedom, and of the balance between preserving individuality and relationality. See Costello, *John Macmurray*, 163–64.

74. John Macmurray, "What About Communism?" *New Britain*, June 14, 1933. Macmurray rarely uses the term "Marxism" and prefers generally to refer to "Marxian" thought or philosophy.

75. Macmurray, "What About Communism?" 14.

76. Macmurray, "What About Communism?" 14.

77. Macmurray, "What About Communism?" 14.

78. John Macmurray, "Equality," *New Britain*, June 21, 1933, 135.

79. Macmurray, "Equality," 135.

80. Macmurray, *Freedom in the Modern World*, 215.

3

MACMURRAY'S ENGAGEMENT WITH MARXIAN THOUGHT IN THE 1930s

Macmurray's fascination with Marx was probably based on his view that Marx was, at bottom, concerned with our estrangement from our own fundamental reality and our ultimate reconciliation with that reality under the appropriate social, economic, and political conditions. In the early 1930s, Macmurray said that Marx was "describing . . . the estrangement [*Entfremdung* or alienation] of Man from himself, from his own reality; and the establishment of communism as the reconciliation of man with himself."[1] Marx's concern with the conditions that give rise to alienation and the recovery of the self parallels Macmurray's concern with achieving the reality of the self. I believe Macmurray came to his concern prior to reading Marx, but certainly the parallels and correspondences in their agendas must have made Macmurray's reading of Marx a confirmation of his own burgeoning ideas.

We know that A. D. Lindsay, Macmurray's tutor at Balliol, had been interested in Marx as early as 1922 and published a book on *Das Kapital* in 1925.[2] So Macmurray would have known something of Marx's work from his days as a student at Oxford. As the decade of the 1930s opened, Macmurray took a new position as Grote Professor of Philosophy and Mind and Logic at University College, University of London. Macmurray was the first English scholar to make use of the 1932 collection of Marx's early writings in the Landshut and Meyer publication of *Der Historische Materialismus: Die Fruhschriften*.[3] He had already confided to friends his ideas about forming "a new social order which would make itself experimentally, on some kind of communist basis, as completely self-contained as possible, and within that framework develops a new type of social life in all its aspects. The governing nucleus of the society—which would be international and federal if possible—should constitute itself a cabinet and lay careful plans for taking over the government of Europe in the event of a collapse of the economic and political machinery."[4] While admitting that the idea was "terribly preposterous," Macmurray followed up with his lengthy analysis of Marx's thought over the course of the decade through a proliferation of books and articles. He was, of course, stepping into a field of study already well-prepared in Great Britain by numerous predecessors interested in, even infatuated with, varieties of socialism and Marxism. Most were confined to, or at least allied with, various versions of Christian socialism and democracy.

In the fall of 1932, Macmurray was invited to attend a conference on the subject "What is Christianity?" that included his old tutor, A. D. Lindsay, John Middleton Murry (a friend of D. H. Lawrence and a student of English literature who was at the time a communist), and several others. As a result of their conversation about Christianity on the first day, they determined that they needed to study two other questions, the nature of modern communism and the problem of sex.[5] Macmurray later confessed that it was this conference that led him to the study of the early works of Karl Marx "with an eye to discovering, in particular, the historical relation between Marxism and the Christian tradition."[6] He went on to assert that he was "astonished" how close the relation between Marxism and the Christian tradition turned out to be. He became convinced that Marx was correct in rejecting any form of religion that was idealistic, world denying, and unreal.

How, he wondered, did religion, Christianity in particular, get so sidetracked from its original mission of establishing the Kingdom of God *on earth*? Part of the explanation, according to Macmurray, was the influence of Platonic philosophy on early Christian thought. Another part of the explanation was the development of a hierarchical and authoritarian ecclesiastical institution, modeled on the Roman state. As Christianity became the religion of the state, its focus shifted to the purely spiritual realm, leaving the control of the material dimensions of life to the machinery of the state. In the process of doing so, Christianity lost that part of itself which was concerned with the just distribution of economic goods for living life in this world, not in the next. "It seemed, indeed, that modern Communism might well be that half of Christianity which had been dropped by the Church in favour of an accommodation with Rome. With this [conviction] I was committed to rediscovering a Christianity which is non-idealist."[7]

From the more practical side, his entry into a more detailed study of Marx begins with his interest in the economic crisis facing England, and the world generally. Consistent with his philosophy that all meaningful thought starts from a problem in action, it would be typical of Macmurray to study someone's thought only if he believed it might provide an answer to a practical question, in this case how to resolve the problems of economic justice that exacerbate the problems of living fully and freely in relation to other persons.

In 1931 Macmurray published an article in the *British Weekly* on the upcoming British elections. The piece made an impassioned plea for international action on the economy, echoing the theme of internationalism he had laid down in his 1929 *British Weekly* article on "The Limits of Interference Between Sovereign States." He was also trying to develop a moral critique of economic life based on his growing sense that the heart of human culture has to do with the elevation and enhancement of individual personality in its deepest relations with others.

Macmurray argued that the power of the economy had never been greater: the problem of its use lies "in our moral imbecility, our jealousy and greed, our primitive terrors."[8] The structure of economic life around the world is so "antiquated and unsound . . . that it is rotting and dropping to pieces slowly before our eyes."[9] The solution is to put the finance and commerce of the world "upon a sane and honest basis by international action," the details of which he did not spell out. Noting that while political structures presuppose independent sovereign nation-states, he argued that economic structures are not bound by national borders. "It is impossible to control our economic life through national governments. That is like going on an elephant hunt with a pop-gun. . . . The thought of a number of independent nations each trying to control the whole international trade of the world in its own interest is an appalling one."[10]

Following up on his commitment to "a new social order which would make itself experimentally, on some kind of communist basis," Macmurray devoted himself to a full-length study that he tellingly entitled *The Philosophy of Communism*.[11] The emphasis on philosophy rather than practice reflected Macmurray's inclination to dig below the surface of various social practices to discover the underlying rationale behind them. Consistent with the epistemological approach taken earlier in "The Unity of Modern Problems" (1929) and explicated formally in *Interpreting the Universe* (published in 1933, the same year as *The Philosophy of Communism*), Macmurray started with a practical problem: the dictatorship in the Soviet Union was inconsistent with the realization of communism.[12] The task was either to change the philosophy or the practice.

Marx himself, Macmurray claimed, never worked out a philosophical theory as such, though he was a brilliant philosopher. Marx's immediate philosophical debt was to Hegel's organic dialectic. This dialectic assumes that all organic processes are dialectical, that reality is an organic process, and that reality is ultimately idea.[13] Marx accepted the first assumption and clearly rejected the third. Orthodox communism accepts the second and interprets it in material terms. Reliance on an organic conception of reality was at the heart of Marxian thought's failure to adequately address the pressing problems of the day. Therefore a new metaphysical scheme was called for. "It might be possible to supply an alternative metaphysical principle which would yield a different metaphysical system and yet be in accordance with his [Marx's] social doctrines," Macmurray argued.[14] That alternative metaphysical principle, of course, is the superorganic reality of persons who cannot be reduced to (even though they contain) the organic dimension.

One thing that helped Marx maintain some conceptual distance from reductionist organicism was his commitment to rejecting idealism (the third of the Hegelian assumptions). Marx had accepted what Macmurray came to on his own: the primacy of action over thought. This was their most decisive break from Hegel, who held that reality is idea. All of them accepted freedom as the goal of reality, but Hegel located freedom in the splendid self-isolation and self-sufficiency of absolute thought. Macmurray and Marx wanted to find it in the field of personal relations. Macmurray believed that Marx "accepted the principle that it is freedom that we are after, and so took his stand firmly in the democratic tradition. . . . But he added that . . . personal reality is essentially social, that it is the reality of personal relationships in society, and further, that what determines the relation of persons in society is the economic reality which they face."[15]

MACMURRAY AND HEGEL

Macmurray and Marx were both deeply indebted to the thought of Hegel. Despite his repudiation of Hegel's organic understanding of social life and what he took to be the totalitarian implications of his political philosophy, Macmurray drew more heavily on Hegel than he admitted in his published works. In particular he adopted from Hegel the idea that only in a social union can the individual find the fulfillment of individual freedom. While skeptical of Hegel's notion of the state, Macmurray agreed that individuals must be brought into harmonious relation with each other if their fulfillment as persons is to be achieved. In *The Philosophy of Right*, Hegel argues that "freedom consists in this, that personal individuality and its particular interests not only achieve their complete development and gain explicit recognition for their right (as they do in the sphere of the family and civil society) but . . . they also pass over of their own accord into the interest of the universal, and, for another thing, they know and will the universal; they even recognize it as their own substantive mind. . . . The result is that the universal does not prevail or achieve completion except along with particular interests and through the co-operation of particular knowing and willing; and individuals likewise do not live as private persons for their ends alone, but in the very act of willing these they will the universal in light of the universal, and their activity is consciously aimed at none but the universal end."[16]

If one substitutes Macmurray's "community" for Hegel's "state," one can see congruence with Macmurray's notion that only by subordinating one's will to what God has intended for all human persons can one achieve the fulfillment of one's personality, including the success of one's freedom of action. If one chooses to act against God's will (and therefore against one's own nature), one cannot be truly free because one is opposing not only what is in one's ultimate best interests but also the very structures and laws of reality.

For Macmurray, a universal community is in one's best interests; it thus makes sense, in Hegel's words, to "know and will the universal" of God's intention. Like Hegel, Macmurray believed that the universal (in this case, the universal community) must provide an important place for, again using Hegel's terminology, the "concrete freedom" of individual and "personal individuality." Clearly Macmurray agreed with Hegel that "individuals do not live as private persons for their own ends alone." Only as communal persons can they live fully—without, of course, sacrificing their unique individualities in the process.

At the same time, Macmurray wanted to stress the importance of the individual members of the unity, and not simply the unity itself as the synthesis of individual and totality. Macmurray was extremely leery of the state functioning as the locus of unity, instead of a community of free individuals each choosing freely to enter into relationships of mutual love and trust with other individuals. And, like Marx, he saw ultimate unity not as a unity of mind, but rather as a unity of action.

Macmurray wanted to avoid falling into Hegelian notions of "organic totality" (which border on totalitarianism), or notions of the independent substantiality of family or society. Hegel, it must be acknowledged, did not think that the individual particularities of the self, including its freedom, ought to disappear into the totality of the state. Rather, he thought that true freedom could only be found by aligning one's will with that of the state.

As distinguished Hegelian scholar J. N. Findlay (for whom Macmurray had served as tutor at Oxford in his years at Balliol) put it: "Hegel insists that the Modern State . . . must allow 'freedom to its particularity,' and must consider the well-being of individuals, and protect their private rights. The State cannot achieve its universal status without the understanding co-operation of groups and individuals, whose subjectivity and 'inwardness' must be allowed to develop in the fullest and most lively manner."[17] Or as Jerry Muller has recently argued, for Hegel "a good life . . . is one in which we are formed by institutions into self-conscious individuals, and into responsible members of institutions that we value because we understand that in the long run they function to make us into the sort of people we want to be."[18] The emphasis here is on conforming the individual's will to the institution, or organization, of the state, not to another person or community (as distinct from society) of persons.

Macmurray's religious commitment to the individual as a free agent standing in chosen relationship with others (including God) also stood in opposition to any loss of the self in a larger totalistic organism, whether it be the state or mind. Nevertheless, he took over from Hegel the underlying idea that the individual and the group of which he or she is a part must ultimately be reconciled. For Macmurray, the means of reconciliation was not the state but the actions of God, who has created humans in such a way that we cannot be fully ourselves independent of the deepest possible relationships of mutuality and love of others in what Macmurray called community. Community requires a degree of individual freedom that is hard to defend in the organic totality model developed by Hegel. God, for Macmurray, is far more capable of grounding human freedom than is a less-than-personal institution such as the state. In this respect, then, Hegel's attempt to reconcile the individual to the state was far less successful than Macmurray's attempt to reconcile humans to a divine personal "other" who, by virtue of its common personhood with them, can bring out and fulfill in human beings all the elements, including freedom, that constitute personhood. Hegel, constrained by the limits of the organic model of unity, failed to see beyond the mechanisms of social organization or the state to a higher form of social unity grounded in the uniquely personal dimensions of human life. He found the reconciliation of individual freedom and relation with others in the wrong place.

This does not mean that Macmurray avoided his own version of totalitarianism. In a remarkably candid analysis of the kind of social unity that constituted the ancient Jewish society and that he thought would constitute the Kingdom of Heaven, he says: "The Jewish people were a totalitarian society—as any religious people must be. The Kingdom of Heaven must be totalitarian, and only a religious society can achieve totalitarian unity."[19] This remarkable claim is qualified, however, by his equally important belief that the kind of totalitarianism he is suggesting is one that can be achieved only through the fundamental principles of human social unity: personal equality and individual freedom. It is a totalitarianism that claims the whole (or total) person as created by God for mutual relationality. As such, it requires the full, free consent of the persons in relation. It is not, therefore, a unity imposed or coerced from outside the self: it is a unity that emerges freely from the self seeking to unify itself not only with itself but with as many personal others as possible in the context of mutual relations. In a *community*, the self is fully itself only when it is appreciated and enjoyed for itself as such, in mutuality and love. The false kind of totalitarianism, Macmurray argued, is "the claim of the State (as organized Society) to use its citizens, in the whole of their human capacity, as means to State-ends. Institutions, organizations, the form of life, become the end of life." And religious socialism must be, in this respect, "fundamentally anti-totalitarian. . . . The organization of society is for the sake of life, not life for the sake of the organization of society. Equality without freedom is as hopeless as freedom without equality."[20]

Despite this fundamental disagreement with Hegel over what constitutes totality, Macmurray would later utilize the Hegelian dialectical phrases "positive" and "negative" as phases in the developed unity of person, society, and community. In reading Macmurray, these phrases are often more distracting than illuminating, but they are an attempt to suggest that practical unity among persons is the result of a process in which a dialectical relationship between its stages is necessary. Hegel gives a primary place to the family (as Macmurray will also do), specifically as it is characterized by love.[21] The family integrates the self as individual and the self as member of a whole greater than itself. But Hegel goes on to define the family as "a" person in a way that Macmurray will not do. Ultimately, for Hegel, civil society "tears the individual from his family ties." And, in its character as "a universal family," society "substitutes its own soil and subjects the permanent existence of even the entire family to dependence on itself and to contingency."[22] Macmurray refrains from tearing individuals from their family ties in order to make them subservient to civil society. In fact, for him, civil society is ultimately to be made subservient to community, of which the family is an original, but not necessarily final or perfect, model.

THEORY AND PRACTICE

Macmurray and Marx, therefore, both relied on and deviated from a Hegelian framework. A more detailed examination of Marxian theory reveals that, for Marx, theory and practice were one. Macmurray claimed that "this principle is the revolutionary principle of community philosophy."[23] It means that theory and practice ought to agree with one another. A theory that does not harmonize with practice is dangerous. Macmurray says succinctly: "Ideas are the eyes of action."[24] But ideas ripped out of their social context are utopian. If I become a utopian thinker, falsely believing that "society is plastic in my hands, as if I were God making the world afresh, [that] I can lift myself out of the stream of history and . . . come down from the clouds and push the world-process in the direction I would like it to go,"[25] then I have fallen into the fallacy of "idealism," which both Marx and Macmurray were at pains to combat.

What we have to deal with, Macmurray argues, if society is to take concrete forms that enhance human life, is a change in social form, that is, "a gradual change in the form of human relationships."[26] Once again the theme of life beyond politics—life that politics and economics and all the organizations of the government are to serve—appeared in Macmurray's work and continued to be the consistent thread on which all his political analysis was based, including his interpretation of Marxian thought.

Marx, he believed, is interested in providing the material, mainly economic, substance that any viable form of human relationships must have. At the heart of the societal struggle is the ownership of the means of the production of these economic resources. Until that struggle is resolved satisfactorily, human action will be stymied: "the problem of freedom is a problem of the control of the material conditions of human action."[27]

In his critique of Marxian philosophy, Macmurray first allied himself emphatically with the rejection of idealism and the principle of the unity of theory and practice.[28] This meant that Macmurray accepted the notion that all theories must be verified in action and be open to experimentation. It also meant a refusal to demand certainty—a demand that is a reflection of the demand for security that, based as it is on fear of the other, leads to the struggle for power between persons and nations. It therefore follows, he asserted, that "any social or philosophical theory which we can then accept, must be either the Marxian theory or some development of the Marxian theory through a process of criticism which falls within the general principles upon which a Marxian theory is based."[29]

The problem with the Marxian theory is the original Hegelian assumption on which it rests; namely, that reality is an organic process. Macmurray reminded his readers that there are three models of relationship: (1) mechanical, or material; (2) organic; and (3) superorganic, or personal.[30] Even social relationships that are cooperative can still fall within the organic model. But the third model of relationship is one in which persons as persons relate to each other, of which friendship is a special example. These relationships are not, strictly speaking, dialectical.[31] They are, in their essential nature, eternal. Contrary to Marx, Macmurray claimed that "they remain essentially the same in form under any conditions of social life. And they do this because they are the ultimate expressions of what human nature essentially is, quite apart from the particular forms of organization which make up the complex of society under the special conditions of any place or any epoch."[32]

Marx is a marvelous interpreter of the organic aspect of human life, especially in its political and economic forms. But an organic interpretation assumes that the organic process, in which social adaptation to the external environment is the essential characteristic, will continue forever. The communist believes that the process is essentially a struggle between social classes over who will control the means of production. He also believes that this struggle will inevitably result in a classless society. And when this happens, the organic dialectic will come to an end. At this point, the organic model will cease to function as an appropriate way of understanding human social relationships. If Marx really believed that true history would begin with the achievement of communism, then, Macmurray argued, he has begun to reject the applicability of the organic model for *all* human relationships, especially those after the establishment of communism. To the extent that we can take control of the organic process, we transcend it. And when we do, human development "ceases to be merely an organic process and becomes superorganic."[33] Through our reason, we have the capability (which we do not always exercise) of escaping from a purely organic understanding of reality and beginning to take control over the planning of a society built on the principles of equality and justice. Macmurray believed that a communist society is one in which this kind of rational planning of social development is possible. Under communism, we would be "free from the absolute necessity to be controlled in the structure of our social life by our material environment."[34] The struggle for power would cease and co-operation would begin.

This, of course, is an analysis at the theoretical level, as Macmurray promised it would be by calling it the "philosophy" of communism. Nevertheless,

Macmurray at a practical level was highly critical of the dictatorship of the Communist Party in the Soviet Union and its unjustified reliance on the mechanisms of the state to enforce its will. He was also critical, however, of capitalism, because he believed it was fundamentally incompatible with democracy. The democratic state in Great Britain had gone overboard in believing that the solution to its problems was purely economic and that politics should be destroyed "in the interests of a state-form which is purely economic and administrative." This is the beginning of fascism, in which politics is swallowed up in economics.[35] Politics ought to be "that field of social organization which exists to secure to men and women their rights as human beings against the impact of powers and forces which do not recognize their humanity. Politics is the field of the perpetual struggle of right against power, or reason and justice against naked force."[36] And, to echo what he had written in "Equality," he concluded that "the recognition of equality is the basis of justice and law."[37]

As one might expect, he ended his study of the philosophy of communism by returning to his emerging notion of community as that which transcends material, utilitarian organizational relations between individuals. *Individualism*, setting the individual apart from others in a state of independence or self-sufficiency, is a false view of the person because it undercuts the essential social relationship all persons ought to have if they are to be real and fulfilled. *Individuality* is the confirmation and expression of the uniqueness of the individual, but it can only occur and be sustained in community.

Women in particular, Macmurray argued, need to free themselves from the false constraints placed on them in the coerced form of family in which they have been subordinated to the needs and desires of husbands, fathers, and brothers. They have a right to insist on their individual integrity and independence (i.e., an identity not determined *for* them by others). This can only happen in a "form of community life which is compatible with the individuality of all its members. . . . Individualism and communism are opposites and irreconcilable. Individuality and community are correlatives."[38]

The Philosophy of Communism received mixed reviews. John Laird (professor of logic and metaphysics at Queens University, Belfast) called Macmurray's presentation of ideas "penetrating, electrifying, and even shrewd—despite his philosophy. In my judgment he is the most stimulating of all contemporary British sociological authors."[39] Clinton Rossiter, a conservative political thinker in the United States, called Macmurray, on the basis of the book, a "British Marxist" and confused Macmurray's treatment of the dialectic in Hegel with his treatment of it in Marx.[40] The most confused critique of the book was provided by T. A. Jackson, apparently an avowed communist, in his book *Dialectics: The Logic of Marxism and Its Critics*.[41] Jackson praised Macmurray for not being a typical British detractor of Marx and appreciated his understanding of the latter's unity of theory and practice. Nevertheless, Macmurray's attempt to go beyond the organic categories of both Hegel and Marx was faulted by Jackson for being a relapse in a "species of modified Hegelianism."[42] He also accused Macmurray of being an idealist, of rejecting the actions of the masses, and of ignoring the "whole teaching of Marxism in respect of class struggle."[43] It is hard to imagine a more total misreading of Macmurray, but Jackson's criticism does indicate that some communist thinkers were taking his ideas seriously.

At virtually the same time that *The Philosophy of Communism* appeared, Macmurray contributed four essays to a book entitled *Some Makers of the Modern Spirit*.[44] The essays were based on twelve BBC talks Macmurray gave in the spring of 1933. In the initial essay, Macmurray claimed that the central thesis of the modern spirit, established by Martin Luther, is "the right of the individual to worship God in his own way."[45] In a subsequent essay, he went on to claim that two ideas lie behind the whole course of modern history: the freedom of the individual, and the equality of all persons.[46] In his final essay, he argued that although science is a useful instrument for understanding the world, in the end it is religion alone that can unify the human spirit, both individually and socially. Religion ought to challenge the constraints of tradition and its institutions. But the freedom to challenge the past has also brought with it glaring discrepancies between rich and poor. These have, in turn, produced a new kind of unfreedom, "the tyranny of the plutocrats, the dictatorship of wealth."[47] Does this mean that we should abandon our freedom, since it can be so easily abused? Macmurray's answer was to refer to Marx's refusal to abandon freedom because "the struggle for freedom and equal freedom against the authority of wealth would prove the final assault by the forces of freedom against the citadel of the enemy."[48] If the struggle is to be won, Macmurray argued, it cannot be through fascism, only through socialism that "reasserts the faith in freedom and equality, and demands that we shall not call a halt and retrace our steps, but carry the struggle through to the bitter end."[49]

In early 1934, Macmurray contributed an article, "The Challenge of Communism," to a book coauthored with Professor H. G. Wood for the Industrial Christian Fellowship.[50] Among other things, Macmurray criticized the traditional Christian practice of private charity for the poor when their situation could only be met realistically with "simple justice."[51] He also acknowledged that in both practice and theory, communists are anti-religious and anti-Christian. He criticized the critics of Christianity for comparing religious ideals with actual practice. This, he argues, was unfair. Like must be compared to like. If you compare philosophy with philosophy, you will find that "in one form or another all the main Communist conceptions, the driving force of the Communist Revolution, are to be found in the teaching in Jesus." These include Jesus' class consciousness ("How hard it is for a rich man to go into the kingdom of heaven"), his economic interpretation of the social problem ("Go, sell what you have and give to the poor"), and his materialism (a man "shall receive a hundredfold now in this time").[52] He did not call for a Marxian communism, but a Christian communism. The Christianity the communists repudiate (in its idealist form) he too wanted to do away with. In the end, the only true test of genuine Christianity is its fruit: whether it ushers in a worldly Kingdom of God characterized by both justice and love.[53]

In the fall of 1934, Macmurray sought to develop his anti-idealism and his commitment to personal freedom in a series of BBC talks that were later printed as "Personality, Freedom and Authority."[54] Freedom, he claimed, is what we are all after. It is the criterion by which we should value any form of social life. The particular kind of freedom he was talking about, however, is the freedom to be as fully and completely the person it is possible for one to be or become: "freedom is being able to be oneself."[55] This right to freedom belongs to persons simply by virtue of their being persons, not by virtue of being members of a particular society or state. And yet, freedom must be won through the appropriate exercise of power in a "very hard real solid world which has its own nature and its own ways of behaving."[56] This is the realism Macmurray believed most traditional forms of religion have shunned in their delusionary search for a spiritual and idealistic solution to human problems. The world does not, in its concrete reality, provide total or unlimited freedom to individuals. The struggle to be fully human must find ways to carve out or extend the limited freedom that the world permits. That struggle, to be successful, must be primarily social, through the cooperation and the interdependence of persons. We cannot be fully free unless others (who stand as real objects in our field of action) make that freedom possible by cooperating with us. Some restrictions on individual freedom may ultimately make more freedom for all possible. Government can either increase freedom by appropriate restrictions or it can diminish it. If lack of material resources inhibits our freedom to be ourselves, then government can place restrictions on the accumulation of resources by some at the expense of others and thus increase the possibility of freedom for all. "There is no way in which freedom can be assured to a man without putting him in possession of the material means by which he can live the full life of human personality."[57]

In the second talk in the series, Macmurray became more explicitly political. He noted that the development of the industrial and financial system was becoming increasingly incompatible with political democracy. He also linked democracy directly with Christianity because at the roots of democracy "there lies, as a fundamental religious principle, that all rightful authority is limited."[58] This is the principle of the absolute value of the human person. The essence of what it means to be human is to be able to make one's own choices and to take responsibility for them. This means that in the political realm, all authority must be limited and judged by its usefulness in sustaining and extending human freedom. This is precisely what is threatened by a totalitarian state, wherein the state claims absolute authority over its citizens. Democracy is the practice of limited authority. Its organizational forms are devised to achieve the purpose of enhancing human freedom. "What makes any form of government democratic is its efficiency in keeping authority within the limits set for it by the democratic principle and in making authority function properly within these limits."[59]

One crucial implication of this political philosophy for Macmurray was that economics lies within the scope of political authority. The freedom of persons depends on their access to material goods equitably distributed. This requires that public authority must "assume control of the economic and financial activities of society."[60] Unlimited freedom for individuals in the economic field results in diminished freedom for many others. "I have no manner of doubt in my own mind that this means that we [must] accept socialism, and accept it fully. With that choice, I am convinced, the whole future of England, of Europe, and of Christianity is bound up. . . . [We must choose either] to create a free social community; or we shall turn our backs on all that is worthy of worship in our past, and descend with chains about our ankles into the dim and shameful slavery of the Totalitarian State."[61]

CHRISTIANITY, MARX, AND COMMUNISM

In 1935 Macmurray continued to develop his interest in and understanding of Marx. One of his first essays to receive significant critical attention was in the book *Marxism*, edited by John Middleton Murry, which emerged from a symposium with Murry and G. D. H. Cole devoted to the relation of Christianity and Marxism.[62]

Several additional relevant writings were published in 1935. He wrote a piece titled "Dialectical Materialism as a Philosophy" for *Aspects of Dialectical Materialism*,[63] edited by H. Levy. He also published *Reason and Emotion*, drawn from BBC lectures.[64] Another full-length manuscript, *Creative Society: A Study of the Relation of Christianity to Communism*, also appeared.[65] "The Dualism of Mind and Matter" appeared in the journal *Philosophy*.[66] Perhaps most importantly, two essays on Marx and Christianity—"The Early Development of Marx's Thought" and "Christianity and Communism: Towards a Synthesis"—appeared in *Christianity and the Social Revolution*, a book edited by John Lewis and others.[67]

Because in all of these Macmurray was trying to develop themes that link Christianity and Marxian thought, I will treat them as a single whole. As he had done in *The Philosophy of Communism* two years earlier (1933), Macmurray wanted to separate Marx's own thought from the deterministic, mechanical straight-jacket that forms of dialectical materialism had taken by the mid-1930s. He claimed throughout that he was not a communist and did not accept "orthodox" communist philosophy.[68] Nevertheless, he found he could accept on philosophical grounds some aspects of dialectical materialism while rejecting others. Although adopted by the Communist Party as an orthodox position, dialectical materialism is, Macmurray argued, more a tendency of thought than a strict philosophy. Marx's own thought, he contended, was much wider, more subtle, and more insightful than this orthodox version of dialectical materialism that has "often become dogmatic where Marx was empirical and superficial where Marx was profound."[69] As such, it misrepresented a movement in history that was working for a truly egalitarian international social order. Marx was right in believing that Hegel's dialectical idealism (which culminates in idea, not in practice) needed to be opposed by an antithesis, namely dialectical materialism (which Macmurray prefers to call "historical critical activity" applied to the sociological field, not the field of ideas).[70] Marx believed that there was a contradiction between what one could become (i.e., "species being") and what one presently was (alienated or estranged from oneself, others, and the products of one's labor) under the prevailing historical conditions of capitalism. The theoretical analysis of that contradiction constituted the dialectic. The dialectic is human reflection upon the tensions and contradictions taking place in history as societies of persons try to adapt themselves to changed conditions. Old ideologies frustrate the emergence of new forms of social relationships. The established ideologies represent the interests of the most powerful class in society, and this is the basis of class struggle.[71]

While appreciating this truth in Marx's understanding of the dialectic, Macmurray also held that dialectical materialism in the hands of orthodox communists winds up with a view of society as nothing more than a reflection of its economic organization. In this respect, it lies at the foundation of fascism.[72] At the same time, orthodox dialectical materialism forgets one of the basic insights of Marx: that all social thought is socially conditioned. Dialectical materialism is no exception to this rule: it will eventually generate its own antithesis. One of the reasons for this is its reliance on an organic conception of society. Dialectical materialism fails to do justice to the freedom of the person in relationships that transcend the economic. We are each subordinated to being a functioning part of an organic whole that is greater and more important than ourselves. Any political philosophy built on the organic model[73] "will tend to think of the individual as existing only in and for the society as a whole, and performing a special function for society. . . . [I]n biology it is the species which is the unit rather than the individuals which make up the species. . . . Thus, all organic philosophies . . . will miss in their interpretation of human life precisely what distinguishes it from sub-human life. The uniqueness of the individual will disappear from sight."[74]

One part of the dialectic that Macmurray did find attractive was its "materialism." By this Macmurray meant that in the unity of theory and practice, it is our struggle with nature that gives rise to reflection as we seek to negotiate our way around the world. If we don't recognize the unity (not the identity) of thought and action, we will be tempted to adopt a dualism between mind and matter or body and soul, a dualism Macmurray questioned in his article "The Dualism of Mind and Matter." The more natural tendency would be a division of reality into animate, inanimate, and personal things. The division into mental and physical is a product of a much greater degree of metaphysical reflection.[75] Mind-body dualism denies that we are persons who have the capacity of knowing ourselves in two different ways. If we are one person, then we know that one aspect of who we are is material (the body) and that it is guided by another part of who we are (our intentions), and that both are integrated into a unified whole in the relation of theory and practice.

If we understand that uniquely human action is intentional action, we overcome the false dualism between mind and matter. Then, and only then, are we in a position to understand that true materialism "means the recognition that the primary distinction to which the dualism of mind and matter crudely refers is between action which is blind and action which is fully conscious. The materialist is the man who knows what he is doing, the man who acts with a full consciousness of why he acts in that way and of what the consequences will be."[76] Idealists, however, are unaware of the real relation between what they think and what they do. The materialist is the one who insists that action is what counts "and all action is necessarily material."[77] According to Macmurray, "We act as bodies upon bodies, and the Marxian materialism is a recognition of this fact. The demand for such a materialism is a demand not for a lower consciousness and a lower form of life but for a fuller consciousness, a higher type of knowledge, a deeper insight into the meaning and significance of human life."[78]

Although this deeper significance is not reducible to the economic, all persons require certain basic necessities for living the full life. These include food, clothing, and shelter. Macmurray added that in a dualistic mentality, people have sought to justify the domination of black persons by whites, and of women by men.[79] In a lengthy statement that exuded the kind of optimism (some would say utopianism) of many quasi-Marxian thinkers, Macmurray argued that the new materialism "sustains the belief that it is possible to construct a universal society of men and women who shall all be free and equal, without distinction of race or nationality. It leads to the conviction that given proper conditions of life men and women everywhere will live in peace and justice and mutual sympathy throughout the world, that it is possible to put an end to the exploitation of men by men, of class by class, of nation by nation, of black man by white man, of the female by the male. It inspires a faith in the redemption of the criminal by kindness, in the possibility of putting an end to poverty, in a future within our grasp in which oppression shall have ceased, and even the State, with its government of men by men, shall have withered away."[80]

To achieve this admittedly somewhat utopian ideal (Macmurray admits that true materialism has "ideals" in the sense of aspirations and goals) requires an appropriate realistic relationship between social relations and their material infrastructure. "No society can exist except in a form which provides for the basic, material needs of human life."[81] A genuine materialism (what Macmurray calls the "new" materialism) is one in which the materialist does not seek to abolish ideals (goals) but "is primarily concerned with the material conditions of their realization."[82]

Paradoxically perhaps, acknowledging the material dimension of human life is a crucial step toward a better understanding of religion, according to Macmurray (in a move that clearly separates him from Marx). A genuine materialism of the sort embraced by Marx can help to restore the true meaning of religion, or at least of the Christianity that is drawn from Judaism. True religion, according to Macmurray, must address these material needs and not spiritualize them in an illusory or idealistic form. Marx focused almost exclusively on the idealistic form of religion, and thus missed what Macmurray regarded as its real or authentic nature. Marx was right in criticizing religion in its idealistic mode, but a synthesis between his negative view of idealistic religion and that of genuine "material" religion is, according to Macmurray, the next necessary dialectical step.

Macmurray undoubtedly knew Marx's critique of religion in the latter's "Contribution to the Critique of Hegel's Philosophy of Right" even though he did not specifically refer to it. There Marx argued that religion in its present historical form (under the conditions of the alienation endemic to capitalism) is an expression of real human distress. But it is only an expression, not a solution: it provides an illusory happiness (in the spiritual world) for real suffering in the material world. It is an illusion because it does not address the material conditions that give rise to suffering in the first place and the psychological responses people make to that suffering when they do not have the political and economic tools to eradicate the source of the pain. (And in this sense religion is an opiate, designed to ease the pain without addressing its underlying causes). For Marx, of course, one cannot get rid of religion until one comes to accept as one's highest goal the restoration of oneself to oneself (the overcoming of alienation, the return to one's "species being"). Thus, according to Marx, the criticism of religion as a false utopian opiate "ends with the teaching that man is the highest essence for man, hence with the categoric imperative to overthrow all relations in which man is a debased, enslaved, abandoned, despicable essence."[83] Until the overthrow happens, religion (in its idealistic and illusionary form) will remain as the "the sigh of the oppressed creature, the heart of a heartless world."[84]

For Macmurray, who clearly retained a positive understanding of religion, the struggle for changing the material conditions of human life is part of what it means to realize the Kingdom of God on earth. True religion requires the abolition of a notion of heaven as "another world" in which the wrongs of this world are corrected. The dualism between spirit and matter must be overcome. The "realization of religion involves the destruction of that ideal world of spiritual blessedness which exists in the mind of the believer in virtue of its separation from, and contrast to, his earthly life."[85] And this meant for Macmurray the "disappearance of [idealist] Christianity as a religion."[86] Macmurray acknowledged that until historical conditions make it possible for human action to bring about a new form of society that will diminish the gap between one's actual life and one's "essential nature," religion will be exploited by those who wish to avoid dealing with the transformation of society. Fortunately, he argued, "when the point in the development of human society is reached at which the mastery of the conditions of life is sufficient to allow of a form of social life which corresponds with the essential nature of humanity, there will no longer be a need for diverting men's minds from the actual life they lead [i.e., alienation] to an ideal world. The social need for an escape-mechanism will have disappeared."[87] But there is a non-idealistic way of understanding religion,[88] and that is what Macmurray took up in his attempt to synthesize Christianity and communism.

At the heart of this synthesis was his conviction that true Christianity is about human community in this world. Because "the true reference of religion is to the field of direct human relationships," it is not possible to cure the problems of human life "by a spiritual regeneration that leaves the organization of economic society out of account. Love in dissociation from hunger is purely sentimental. Hunger in dissociation from love is purely anti-social. The direct and the indirect relations of men in society are inseparable."[89] In short, human beings need the economic and political organizations that comprise the material relations of life (the indirect relations that constitute a society), and they need the direct relations that constitute the fullness of human life in love and mutuality (community). The synthesis must recognize both. Although Macmurray would develop the relation between indirect and direct forms of relationships far more thoroughly in the Gifford Lectures some twenty years later, one hears the fundamental distinction in his work on communism in the 1930s. This distinction is the basis for Macmurray's answer to Kymlicka's original question of what more we need to say about human relationships than can be said in the terms of political philosophy.

Macmurray was already convinced that religion is ultimately and essentially about community, about direct relations of love and trust between individual human beings. Direct relations are not simply organic but personal (or superorganic). They have no purpose or function beyond the intrinsic fulfillment persons find in them. They are "the direct expression of the inherently mutual or communal nature of man."[90] "All religion is the expression of community."[91]

To move into genuine community requires persons to confront the reality of fear. Macmurray believed that true religion is based on the opposite of fear: trust in the power of a reality "that is irresistible and yet friendly" (i.e., God).[92] He criticized communist theory for its rejection of belief in God because, he was convinced, that rejection "makes its understanding of human reality dim and limited, and in practice hampers and diverts its efforts and may, in the long run, frustrate them."[93]

The primordial fear is that of death, because death cuts us off from others. The fear of death is the fear of isolation. (That is why individualism is linked to fear of others, even though it falsely believes that by separating oneself from other persons who can threaten our lives, we are somehow better off.) Religion is the attempt to acknowledge death and to overcome the fear of it through an articulation of the human being's quest for eternal life.[94] Fear isolates us from what we fear. Trust enables us to enter into positive relations with it, to reintegrate us with other persons, and with nature, both of which we fear because they can take our lives. Faith is the term Macmurray used for "that attitude of consciousness which is completely triumphant over fear."[95] Faith is not the ability to believe in ideas (doctrines) that violate or transcend the canons of rationality. It is an aspect of action: a willingness to believe that if one is on the side of reality, one's actions will be ultimately successful.

MACMURRAY'S UNSUCCESSFUL
CRITIQUE OF PRAGMATISM

Macmurray tried to address the question of pragmatism when he discussed the role of action in the world. He seemed to equate pragmatism with a narrow form of opportunism, of using theory as "propaganda without concern for truth."[96] The pragmatist, he believed, identifies the truth of a belief with its "satisfactoriness as a basis for action. Truth is what works." This assumes that the pragmatist believes ideas emerge without any reference to their origin in action. And this is tantamount to a dualism that "vitiates pragmatism completely."[97] Pragmatism, Macmurray argued, has no objective way of determining which results are truly or objectively fulfilling to human nature. "If truth is what works, then social truth is what is expedient for the people to believe."[98] In offering "practical satisfactoriness" as a criterion of truth, pragmatism "strikes at the roots of intellectual honesty and justifies the conservation of comfortable illusions."[99] He seemed to think that practical pragmatism (as distinct from theoretical pragmatism, which allows us to believe whatever makes us happy) justifies the use of propaganda by the state to dehumanize an enemy, or to advance narrow nationalistic goals. Given this very narrow reading of pragmatism, it is not surprising that Macmurray wanted to argue that truth is not always satisfactory. "It is usually disturbing and unwelcome, often tragic and disillusioning; sometimes catastrophic."[100]

It is clear that Macmurray had a profoundly truncated and misleading view of pragmatism, at least of that developed by James, Peirce, and Dewey.

None of them would have argued for the restricted, self-serving form of pragmatism Macmurray was attacking. What he failed to see is that genuine pragmatism and his own work are profoundly at one in their common belief that ideas must be tested by their reliability (not psychological satisfactoriness) in guiding action in the real world. A great deal in John Dewey, for example, parallels Macmurray's own ideas about the relation between theory and practice in the building up of human community.[101] We should not be sidetracked, therefore, by Macmurray's rather ill-informed diatribe against his particular version of pragmatism. Like the genuine pragmatists, he is committed to the view that ideas are ultimately to be tested by their ability to guide action in a way that tracks with reality as it is, or as it can become, not simply with what we would like it to be for selfish reasons.

The question is whether religion tracks with reality in a way that does not deny or frustrate the fulfillment of the human person (what Marx would call one's "species being"). Religion seeks to realize a completely trusting attitude of mind to the world in which one lives and acts. It wants to restore to us the sense of our own value, to free us to trust our own nature.[102] This is what the concept of the forgiveness of sins means and why it is so central in the teaching of Christianity. If one's sins are forgiven, one is freed from the paralysis of guilt. This is what Jesus did, according to Macmurray: by asking God to forgive even those who crucified him, he was seeking to restore to persons their confidence in themselves. Without that confidence, they would be imprisoned by fear and thus unable to enter joyfully into mutual relations with others, through which alone they can be fulfilled as persons.

The human experiences of love and death are eternal and do not disappear even when the social organization of life has reached the apex of justice and equality under communism. The mere achievement of communism will not eliminate these essential components of human life. "The Communist is too apt to think that the form of social organization is the whole of human reality, whereas it is not even its substance."[103] The substance is fellowship and community for its own sake. Here is where Christianity parts company with communism. Personal relations are the essence of human life, not economic relations (as important as the latter are as preconditions for the former). Economic relations are indirect because they are mediated by the exchange of goods. They are relations of cooperation. They can be organized by political actions within an organic framework, since an organism is the successful organization of multiple parts cooperating with one another for the harmonious life of the organism as a whole. With respect to these organic, indirect relations, communism does well. On the other hand, personal relations are direct, mediated only by the "mutual recognition of one another as fellows in the sharing of a common life. . . . They are the direct expression of the inherently mutual or communal nature of man."[104] The failure of communism is to account satisfactorily for this communal nature of the human person. It thus can give no true account of religion, whose field of theory and practice is community.

Communism is, in a sense, the organic, organizational answer to the problem of hunger. Community is the supraorganic answer to the problem of love. Communism responds to the hunger motive, which is "the fundamental source of human co-operation in work for the mastery of matter and the provision for all physical needs."[105] The satisfaction of hunger is one way of responding to the fear of death. It leads each of us to appropriate as much of the world as we can to stave off death and the threat of others who, in our fear, we believe seek to do us harm. (This, Macmurray suggested, is the basis of private property).[106]

Religion responds to the love motive, which seeks not to appropriate the world to the self but to give the self to the world. Love is the "affirmation of the being of another person in one's own conscious life."[107] Communism assumes if it solves the economic problem that allows hunger to persist, it will have solved the human problem. But surely this cannot be right. In fact, only if the hunger problem is solved can the problem of (or better, the potential for) love be solved. Ironically (given Marx's critique of utopianism in others), communism suffers from its own utopianism, because it believes that fulfilled human life is possible without religion.

Strictly speaking, both hunger and love must be addressed, not one to the exclusion of the other. (This is entailed by a denial of dualism between matter and spirit.) Human society is possible only if people cooperate for economic purposes, and such cooperation would be "impossible apart from the impulse to enter into community."[108] Christianity is wrong if it believes that it can look solely to a spiritual renewal of persons that omits sustained attention to the practical economic organization of society. Communism is wrong if it believes that it can look solely to a material organization of economic life that omits attention to the human demand for the superorganic experience of community.[109] This is the synthesis of Christianity and community to which Macmurray directed his attention.

The synthesis between Christianity and communism also requires a dialectical development within Christianity. It must reconcile the insight that human community is initially most fully expressed in small communities with its intention to establish a universal community. This reconciliation can only be possible through a historical process that moves from small to universal community. This will require concrete historical steps, political and economic, to unify humankind. Christianity will have to change as these steps unfold. Christianity must seek to conform the inner life to its outward expression in the most inclusive social organization possible.[110]

NOTES

1. John Macmurray, *Reason and Emotion* (New York: Barnes and Noble, 1962), 65. The book was based on BBC lectures Macmurray gave in 1935.

2. A. D. Lindsay, *Karl Marx's Capital: An Introductory Essay* (London: Oxford University Press, 1925). Lindsay tries to free Marx from the charge that he is a determinist but criticizes his conviction that there can eventually be a harmonization of selfish interests in a collectivist society, calling this view "an optimism only less fatuous" than the alternative view that it can be brought about by capitalist market forces (pp. 43–44). See M. P. Ashley and C. T. Saunders, *Red Oxford: A History of the Growth of Socialism in the University of Oxford* (Oxford: Oxford University Labour Club, 1930). G. D. H. Cole, Lindsay's successor at Oxford as president of the Fabian Society, took a very similar line to his predecessor. In his *What Marx Really Meant* (London: Gollancz, 1934), Cole argued that, for Marx, theory and practice were inextricably linked, thus freeing him from the charge of being a materialist. He was, instead, a realist whose true enemy (as Macmurray himself would argue) was idealism. But he criticized Marx for reducing all historical explanation to the economic and especially for his tendency to explain away religion.

3. Karl Marx, *Der Historische Materialismus: Die Fruhschriften*, herausgegeben von S. Landshut und J. P. Meyer, unter Mitwirkung von F. Salomen (Leipsig: Alfred Kroner Verlag, c. 1932). Most studies of Marx prior to the early 1930s had been based on the *Communist Manifesto* and his *Contribution to the Critique of Political Economy*. The earliest writings of Marx, especially the *Economic and Philosophical Manuscripts of 1844*, did not become available in English until the early 1930s, when Macmurray was busy working with their translation. See Raymond Plant, "Social Thought," in *The Twentieth Century Mind: History, Ideas, and Literature in Britain*, vol. 2, 1918–1945, ed. C. B. Cox and A. E. Dyson (London: Oxford University Press, 1972), 81–82. A contemporary Marxist scholar, Istvan Meszaros, has noted the importance of Macmurray's work on the early Marx and believes Macmurray's awareness of the inseparability of the early and later work of Marx has still not been fully appreciated by contemporary scholars. See Meszaros, *Marx's Theory of Alienation* (London: Merlin Press, 1970), 217–18. (He is referring specifically to a somewhat later piece by Macmurray in *Christianity and the Social Revolution*, which will be taken up below).

4. Letter to Irene Grant, August 1932. Found in John Costello, *John Macmurray: A Biography* (Edinburgh: Floris Books, 2002), 195.

5. John Macmurray, *The Search for Reality in Religion* (London: Quaker Home Service, 1965), 25.

6. Macmurray, *The Search for Reality in Religion*, 25.

7. Macmurray, *The Search for Reality in Religion*, 27.

8. John Macmurray, "The Coming Election," *British Weekly*, October 24, 1931, 1686.

9. Macmurray, "The Coming Election."

10. Macmurray, "The Coming Election."

11. John Macmurray, *The Philosophy of Communism* (London: Faber and Faber, 1933).

12. Macmurray, *The Philosophy of Communism*, 10.

13. Macmurray, *The Philosophy of Communism*, 15.

14. Macmurray, *The Philosophy of Communism*, 18.

15. Macmurray, *The Philosophy of Communism*, 30.

16. *Hegel's Philosophy of Right*, translated with notes by T. M. Knox (New York: Oxford University Press, 1967), 160–61. (Translated from G. W. F. Hegel, *Naturrect und Staatswissenschaft im Grundrisse and Grundlinien der Philosophie des Rechts*, 1821).

17. J. N. Findlay, *Hegel: A Re-Examination* (New York: Collier Books, 1962), 326–27.

18. Jerry Z. Muller, *The Mind and the Market* (New York: Alfred A. Knopf, 2002), 152.

19. John Macmurray, "The Nature of Religion," Report of the St. Asaph Conference, August 1938, 17.

20. John Macmurray, "Russia and Finland," *Christian Left* (March 1940): 6.

21. *Hegel's Philosophy of Right*, 110.

22. *Hegel's Philosophy of Right*, 148.

23. Macmurray, *The Philosophy of Communism*, 36.

24. Macmurray, *The Philosophy of Communism*, 41.

25. Macmurray, *The Philosophy of Communism*, 43.

26. Macmurray, *The Philosophy of Communism*, 46.

27. Macmurray, *The Philosophy of Communism*, 58.

28. Macmurray, *The Philosophy of Communism*, 62.

29. Macmurray, *The Philosophy of Communism*, 63.

30. For my development of this tripartite modeling of social relationships, see my *Community: A Trinity of Models* (Washington, D.C.: Georgetown University Press, 1986).

31. I will argue later on, however, that in the 1950s Macmurray introduces the notion of "resistance" in the development of personal individuality. There is also a notion of "withdrawal and return" in our relation to others when we step out of the immediacy of the relationship from time to time to get a better grasp on what is going on (or failing to go on) in the relationship. These are, I think, shadows or hints of a dialectic, so it does not entirely disappear from Macmurray's thought.

32. Macmurray, *The Philosophy of Communism*, 66.

33. Macmurray, *The Philosophy of Communism*, 72.

34. Macmurray, *The Philosophy of Communism*, 77.

35. Macmurray, *The Philosophy of Communism*, 92.

36. Macmurray, *The Philosophy of Communism*, 92.

37. Macmurray, *The Philosophy of Communism*, 93.

38. Macmurray, *The Philosophy of Communism*, 95–96.

39. John Laird, review of *The Philosophy of Communism* in *Philosophy* 10 (1935): 483.

40. Clinton Rossiter, *Marxism: The View from America* (New York: Harcourt Brace, 1960), 31.

41. T. A. Jackson, *Dialectics: The Logic of Marxism and Its Critics* (London: Lawrence and Wishart, 1936).

42. Jackson, *Dialectics*, 482.

43. Jackson, *Dialectics*, 487.

44. John Macmurray, ed., *Some Makers of the Modern Spirit* (London: Methuen, 1933). The single most prolific year of publication in Macmurray's professional life is 1935.

45. Macmurray, "The Modern Spirit: An Essay," in *Some Makers of the Modern Spirit*, 20.

46. Macmurray, "Introductory," *Some Makers of the Modern Spirit*, 44.

47. Macmurray, "Summary," *Some Makers of the Modern Spirit*, 186.

48. Macmurray, "Summary," *Some Makers of the Modern Spirit*, 187.

49. Macmurray, "Summary," *Some Makers of the Modern Spirit*, 188.

50. John Macmurray, "The Challenge of Communism," in *Christianity and Communism*, ed. H. G. Wood and John Macmurray (London: Industrial Christian Fellowship, 1934), 16–32.

51. Macmurray, "The Challenge of Communism," 16.

52. Macmurray, "The Challenge of Communism," 23.

53. Macmurray, "The Challenge of Communism," 26–27, 32.

54. John Macmurray, "Personality, Freedom and Authority," broadcast October 16, 1934. In typewritten form in the author's personal possession, presumably based on a transcript of the broadcast.

55. Macmurray, "Personality, Freedom and Authority," 1.

56. Macmurray, "Personality, Freedom and Authority," 2.

57. Macmurray, "Personality, Freedom and Authority," 5.

58. Macmurray, "Personality, Freedom and Authority II," 2.

59. Macmurray, "Personality, Freedom and Authority II," 3.

60. Macmurray, "Personality, Freedom and Authority II," 4.

61. Macmurray, "Personality, Freedom and Authority II," 4–5.

62. J. Middleton Murry, ed., *Marxism* (London: Chapman and Hall, 1935).

63. H. Levy et al., *Aspects of Dialectical Materialism* (London: Watts, 1935).

64. John Macmurray, *Reason and Emotion* (New York: Barnes and Noble, 1962).

65. John Macmurray, *Creative Society: A Study of the Relation of Christianity to Communism* (London: SCM Press, 1935).

66. John Macmurray, "The Dualism of Mind and Matter," *Philosophy* 10 (1935): 264–78.

· 67. John Lewis, ed., *Christianity and the Social Revolution* (London: Victor Gollancz, 1935).

68. Macmurray, "Dialectical Materialism as a Philosophy," in Levy, *Aspects of Dialectical Materialism*, 31; and "The Early Development of Marx's Thought," in Lewis, *Christianity and the Social Revolution*, 209.

69. Macmurray, "The Nature of Philosophy," in Murry, *Marxism*, 27.

70. Macmurray, "The Early Development of Marx's Thought," 214.

71. Macmurray, "The Nature and Function of Ideologies," in Murry, *Marxism*, 68–69. While Macmurray rejects the necessity of violent revolution, he does not deny the class struggle. "What makes the class struggle and what determines its issue is the relation between the interests of a class and the general interests of society. . . . [[T]he ruling class] produces conditions in which its own interests are in opposition to the interests of society as a whole. And that situation is one of unstable equilibrium; its development leads to the class-struggle and to revolution." Macmurray, "The Nature and Function of Ideologies," 69.

72. Macmurray, "Dialectical Materialism as a Philosophy," 51.

73. See the fuller development of this concept in chapter 2, and in particular in Macmurray's *Interpreting the Universe*, chap. 5, "Biological Thought and Organism."

74. Macmurray, "Dialectical Materialism as a Philosophy," 44–45.

75. John Macmurray, "The Dualism of Mind and Matter," 267.

76. Macmurray, "The New Materialism," in Murry, *Marxism*, 47.

77. Later Macmurray will admit that even thinking is an activity of the self, because he wants to argue that the self is primarily or essentially an agent, one of whose actions is thinking.

· 78. Macmurray, "The New Materialism," 48.

79. Macmurray remained remarkably free from most of the male superiority or chauvinist views of his time. He wanted genuine equality in all social respects between men and women. More will be said about this side of his thought when we develop the themes of the Gifford Lectures.

80. Macmurray, "The New Materialism," 50 51.

81. Macmurray, "The Nature and Function of Ideologies," 63.

82. Macmurray, "The New Materialism," 51.

· 83. Karl Marx, "Contribution to the Critique of Hegel's Philosophy of Right," Karl Marx and Friedrich Engels, *On Religion*, introduction by Reinhold Niebuhr (New York: Schocken Books, 1964), 50.

84. Marx, "Contribution to the Critique of Hegel's Philosophy of Right," 42.

85. Macmurray, "The Early Development of Marx's Thought," 231.

86. Macmurray, "The Early Development of Marx's Thought," 231.

87. Macmurray, "Christianity and Communism: Towards a Synthesis," *Christianity and the Social Revolution*, 516–17.

88. Macmurray generally tended to identify religion with Judaism and Christianity. It is not clear that he studied deeply or understood much about non-Western, nontheistic religions, and certainly he did not have a well worked out theory about religion as such.

89. John Macmurray, "Christianity and Communism: Towards a Synthesis," 526.

90. John Macmurray, "Christianity and Communism: Towards a Synthesis," 523.

91. Macmurray, *Creative Society*, 32.

92. Macmurray, *Creative Society*, 21. More will be said about the complex and occasionally unclear notion of God found in Macmurray as we develop his fuller philosophy of the personal.

93. Macmurray, *Creative Society*, 28. The notion of "frustration" of effort is taken up more fully in his later work *The Clue to History* (1938).

94. Macmurray, *Creative Society*, 37–38.

95. Macmurray, *Creative Society*, 109.

96. Macmurray, "The New Materialism," 53.

97. Macmurray, "The New Materialism," 54.

98. Macmurray, "The New Materialism," 56.

99. Macmurray, "The New Materialism," 57.

100. Macmurray, "The New Materialism," 56–57.

101. For an illuminating study of the parallels between Macmurray and Dewey, see Robert Johann, *The Pragmatic Meaning of God* (Milwaukee: Marquette University Press, 1966).

102. Macmurray, *Creative Society*, 111.

103. Macmurray, "Christianity and Communism: Towards a Synthesis," 518.

104. Macmurray, "Christianity and Communism: Towards a Synthesis," 522–23.

105. Macmurray, *Creative Society*, 114.

106. Macmurray, *Creative Society*, 114.

107. Macmurray, *Creative Society*, 115.

108. Macmurray, "Christianity and Communism: Towards a Synthesis," 524.

109. Macmurray, "Christianity and Communism: Towards a Synthesis," 526.

110. Macmurray, *Creative Society*, 125.

4

COMMUNITY IN MARX AND MACMURRAY: A REAPPRAISAL

Macmurray's major articles and book on Marx and communism received generally favorable reviews after their publication in 1935.[1] A question that remains from Macmurray's analysis of Marx is whether Marx's understanding of community comes close to the key elements in Macmurray's work on community. I think a case can be made that even within Marx's questionable economic theories and the organic model in which he places them, there is something that points to, without being completely consonant with, Macmurray's understanding of community. The issue is whether Marx's understanding of community can be extracted from the organic totality model in which he tended to couch it without fundamentally distorting it.

At least fifteen years after Macmurray had observed it, the presence of an organic model in Marx was noted by Sidney Hook in 1950.[2] In the 1970s, Melvin Rader called it the "organic totality" model, and Bertell Ollman referred to it as "the theory of internal relations."[3] If Marx's understanding of social life in a postcapitalistic age at least partially transcends the organic model, then there is a possibility that Marx's vision of persons in relations can be reconciled with Macmurray's understanding of community. In order to accomplish this, Marx's conception of community needs to be given more specificity than is usually found by treating it simply as "interdependence" or "cooperation" in contrast with independence and competition. The central claim of Macmurray's model of community is that, as a means to self-realization, mutuality is more than cooperation. Marx's vision of community moves uneasily between these two views.

The question is whether Marx's understanding of community is completely subsumed in functional organic categories or whether it hints at something more, which might find points of contact with a notion of community more explicitly interpersonal, mutual, and *intrinsically* fulfilling. In an organic conception of society, the relations of its members are functional: each plays an allotted part in the achievement of the common end. The society then has an organic form. As Macmurray put it, "it is an organization of functions: and each member is a function of the group."[4] The functional nature of the organic society is its defining characteristic and marks its single most important difference from the more inclusive personal community characterized by mutuality. For Macmurray, the organic form values the individual only with respect to his or her functionality for the other organs constituting the organism as a whole. "Only in functional connection with the other elements has each any being in the whole. Thus the whole value of each element depends upon its subordination, as it were, to the whole complex. . . . The more organic, in fact, society becomes, the more the organic whole absorbs him, willing or unwilling, and sucks the life out of him for its own purpose."[5]

In Marx, cooperative relations are often considered the only alternative to the competitive atomistic relationships dominant in capitalism. Social interdependence is asserted by Marx as a fact that undermines liberalism's insistence on individualism. It seems enough to him simply to note that people do work together and are bound in networks of functional interdependence (through economic, political, social, and psychological ties). The facts of interdependence and the virtues of social cooperation seem sufficient to repudiate the claims of atomistic or radical independence. But they are not the same, in Macmurray's thought, as the mutuality of community. The question is whether Marx has room for a transcooperative mutuality or delight in the other as other, even when it goes beyond functional interdependence.

When Marx focuses on economic relations, it is obvious and perhaps necessary that he does so under an organic model because economic relations are by their nature indirect and impersonal, relations of cooperation, and therefore are functional and organic. To the extent that Marx adopts a dialectical, material understanding of economic relations (and Macmurray is willing to concede that this may not be an unqualified adoption), he commits himself to the thesis that human fulfillment will occur in the development of material conditions exclusively. Communism may in practice have adopted the materialist claims in full, but Marx may not have, Macmurray believes. Nevertheless, the organic model of human relationship lends itself particularly well to a materialist principle. A dialectical process is an organic process in which one phase always succeeds another and no completion or

fulfillment of the whole is possible. Unless Marx has a vision of a postdi-
alectical era in which a unification of the phases of material development
takes place, he will not have entirely escaped an organic understanding of
human relationships as primarily economic.

It is certainly true that Marx understood bourgeois society as an "organic system," which in "its development to its totality consists precisely in
subordinating all elements of society to itself, or in creating out of it the organs which it still lacks."[6] This description perfectly correlates with Macmurray's view of the organism as differentiated and dynamic, and as subordinating all elements within it to the totality of the whole. Melvin Rader,
who claims that Marx's model of bourgeois society is *identical* to the bio-
logical/organic model of the human nervous system, emphasizes the "interdependence of part and part, and part and whole" within the social
organism.[7] Marx also believes that human beings are thoroughly interdependent with nature,[8] suggesting perhaps that dialectical development may
never be able to produce a human experience that goes beyond the organic
processes that characterize nature.

Bertell Ollman stresses the importance for Marx of not distinguishing
the human person from nature. Ollman's theory of "internal relations"
(which he admits was never completely worked out by Marx) takes the organic model to its logical conclusion. Ontologically, he claims, each thing *is*
only a relation to something else, not a thing *in* relation to other things. In
Marx, he claims, "all conjunction is organic, intrinsic to the social units with
which he is concerned and part of the nature of each: . . . interaction is,
properly speaking, *inneraction*," and reciprocity is possible only "because it
occurs within an organic body."[9] According to Ollman, quoting Marx directly from the "Theses on Feuerbach," the human person becomes simply
the "'assemble [aggregate] of social relations.' Elsewhere, this same creature
is said to be 'a natural object, a thing, although a living conscious thing.'
Marx can refer to man as a thing as well as an assemble of social relations,
because he conceives of each as a Relation."[10]

Allen W. Wood reinforces Rader's and Ollman's organic reading of
Marx's understanding of persons-in-relation. Wood focuses on the teleological dimension in the organic model, the process of development toward
some goal. What is significant about Wood's reading is that teleological explanation does not refer to "the intentions of a human or superhuman
agent."[11] An element within a system is teleologically explained when it
"manifests or contributes to the persistent tendencies which characterize the
system" and "exists *because* it manifests or contributes to those tendencies."[12]
Wood then argues that Marx's dialectical materialism relies on teleological

explanation as Marx tries to show that social relations "manifest or contribute" to a society's tendency "to make efficient use of its productive powers."[13] For Wood, Marx's commitment to an organic model is intrinsically wedded to his dialectical theory. "For Marx the world is a system of organically interconnected processes characterized by inherent tendencies to development, and subject periodically to radical changes in organic structure."[14] Dialectical theory views these processes organically, traces their hierarchical structure through the stages of its concreteness, and explains the systematic changes in it by the "developmental tendencies inherent in it."[15]

If Rader, Ollman, and Wood are correct, Marx relies exclusively on organic tendencies that leave no room for human intentional intervention in and transcendence of the organic base necessary for all human action. Society becomes nothing more than a cooperative organic whole in which persons are merely functional organs cooperating for a common end according to "developmental tendencies" built into their nature. A community in which persons deliberately choose to enter into intrinsically delightful, loving relationships cannot be captured in this organic view of social relations. Do Rader, Ollman, and Wood fully capture Marx's thinking on this subject? The answer, I suggest, is ambiguous.

As is clear from the *Economic and Philosophic Manuscripts*, Marx believed that the human person, or "species being," was communal or social, that "society itself produces *man as man*."[16] Communism is described there as "the complete return of man to himself as a *social* (i.e., human) being."[17] Despite Marx's claim not to have an "essentialist" view of human nature, it is clear that for him the nonalienated person is essentially a social being.[18]

But is sociality merely a *fact* and not something to be *intended* as a good in itself? Marx often talks as if the human being's social orientation were simply a given of nature. Other beings, including persons, are objects "indispensable to the manifestation and confirmation of his essential powers. . . . A being which is not itself an object for some third being has no being for its object . . . [and] . . . an unobjective being is a *nullity*—an *un-being*."[19] Marx uses decidedly organic language in referring to "activity in direct association with others" as "an organ for *expressing* my own life, and a mode of appropriating *human* life."[20] This seems to suggest that other persons, as natural objects, function for us in confirming, enriching, and realizing our own self-fulfillment. "My object can only be the confirmation of one of my essential powers."[21] As Ollman puts it, "human beings possess those necessary attributes which enable others to achieve complete fulfillment through them."[22] One does not get a sense here of the mutual delight persons find in working lovingly *for* others. Rather, the emphasis seems to be on the necessity of mutually *using* others for individual self-fulfillment. What distinguishes this view from capitalism is its explicit acknowledgment of social interdependence as the necessary condition for self-fulfillment and its rejection of the capitalist myth of individualism.

Ironically, despite his commitment to a social view of human nature, Marx seems highly suspicious of social relationships that entail *dependence* on another. If for Marx the realization of what Istvan Meszaros calls "human life-activity as internal need"[23] is the highest moral good, then it is not surprising to find Marx stressing the "self-determined" character of self-fulfillment. This self-determination seems to mean being unrestricted by others in the exercise of one's powers. And this means, in true Hegelian spirit, that freedom is actually *independence* from others, being in and for oneself. Eugene Kamenka makes the point this way: "To be free is to be determined by one's own nature. To be unfree is to be determined from without."[24] As Marx says approvingly, "a *being* only considers himself independent when he stands on his own feet; and he only stands on his own feet when he owes his *existence* to himself. A man who lives by the grace of another regards himself as a dependent being."[25] As Kamenka argues, for both Marx and Hegel the logic of the organic model is that the self-determined being "must become . . . the single, all-embracing substance. It is no accident that Marx is forced to take all social institutions, even non-human objects, into man himself, forced to reconcile Subject and Object by obliterating the distinction between them. . . . [I]n the name of . . . the continuity of human and non-human events, Marx has reduced everything to Man,"[26] just as Hegel had reduced it to spirit. It is not coincidental that Hegel develops the full notion of self-determination through the organic totality notion of the absolute. According to Kamenka, Marx ultimately holds that *all* distinctions disappear in the self-determined individual, including the differences between "one man and another."[27] Such a reading of Marx's organic model is perfectly consistent with Ollman's interpretation. Ollman claims to have found that in Marx, "through its internal ties to everything else, each factor is everything else viewed from this particular angle."[28] The only distinctions that count are, appropriately enough given the organic model, *functional* or provisional ones in which things can be given the same names and treated similarly when their function is identical with the function of other things.

The notions of living by the grace of others and of affirming the non-functional worth of each person are at the heart of Macmurray's view of community, in which we go out of ourselves to love others in some measure selflessly simply for *who* they are, not for what they *do*, including what they do for us.[29] Of course, such dependence on the grace of others is understood to be complementary to their enrichment and empowerment *precisely because* each person is intending not self-fulfillment in the first instance but the fulfillment of the others, just as the others, in the web of reciprocal mutuality, intend that person's fulfillment in the first instance. In this way the needs of each will be met by the love of all the others directed heterocentrically, that is, placing the interests of the other (hetero) ahead of the interests of one's own self (ego).[30]

Marx does insist on the necessity of community to achieve personal autonomy. As he says in the *German Ideology*, "only in community[31] [with others has each] individual the means of cultivating his gifts in all directions; only in the community, therefore, is personal freedom possible. . . . The illusory community, in which individuals have up till now combined, always took on an independent [i.e., dualistic] existence in relation to them. . . . In a real community the individuals obtain their freedom in and through their association."[32] Marx clearly intends to reject the kind of (illusory) community in which the individual produces only for selfish ends. In such a community, "I have produced for myself and not for you, as you have produced for yourself and not for me," Marx states; "our production is not a production of men for men as such, that is social production. Thus, as a man none of us is in a position to be able to enjoy the product of another. We are not present to our mutual products as men. . . . Each of us sees in his own product only his own selfish needs objectified."[33]

In this crucial passage from Marx's reflections on James Mill, we get the clearest hint of his attempt to transcend the organic model of functional relationships in the service of self-realization. Here he suggests the possibility of enjoying others for their own sake and not simply as objects useful for one's own sake. The enjoyment of something points to more than its use-value. When alienated production has been transcended and I can produce "in a human manner,"[34] I will be able to objectify my individuality (and thus *enjoy* the expression of my life and of seeing it made objective) and enjoy realizing (upon others' enjoyment of my product) "that I had both satisfied a human need by my work and also objectified the human essence and therefore fashioned for another human being the object that met his need."[35] This is for Marx the heart of mutuality: I enjoy satisfying your need just as you acknowledge and feel me to be "a completion of your own essence and a necessary part of yourself."[36] Marx even employs in this context a term that seems dangerous to many doctrinaire Marxists: "love." He says that, in this mutual relation, I will be "confirmed both in your thought and in your love."[37] "In my expression of my life I would have fashioned your expression of your life, and thus in my own activity have realized my own essence, my human, my communal essence. In that case our products would be like so many mirrors, out of which our essence shone."[38]

This passage is strangely at odds with the organic model. Here persons are not only functionally related but also seem to be objects of love and affirmation, as would be true in what Macmurray calls the "superorganic" mode of relationship. They do not merely relate to one another as cooperative factors only functionally distinguishable (à la Ollman). Their objective in production seems, at least in part, the genuine development of others as unique persons (since each produces in a way that is unique) and subsequently their enjoyment of others' work. Cooperation as a means to one's self-development has taken a backseat to (though not without the aid of) cooperation as a means to the intrinsic good of the self-fulfillment of all others, who also intend one's own fulfillment. In such a relationship of mutuality one is, in a real sense, dependent on the grace (a term Marx would probably not use, of course) of others. But in this context, such dependence is implicitly nonproblematic, since the exercise of one's grace will be *for* others' development, not simply for oneself through the use of others.

If this reading of Marx's notion of community is correct, why has it traditionally been subordinated to more materialistic, deterministic, and organic readings? The answer, I think, is simply that Marx focused most of his attention on the overcoming of a society of persons alienated, due to the conditions of capitalism, from each other, from the product of their labor, and from themselves. Capitalism was thoroughly organic despite the ideological disguise it tried to assume. In order to supercede capitalism, one had to understand it in its own terms and confront its actual conditions without the luxury of ideological retreat into a dream world of communism before it could be put into practice. To dwell on what could easily be taken for utopian fantasies would have been counterproductive. Marx insisted that the resolution of contradictions inherent in capitalism would occur not primarily in theory but in practice (*praxis*). Until political, even revolutionary, attempts could be made, consistent with the appropriate stage of historical and material conditions, to bring down capitalism and begin its replacement through the stages of socialism and eventually communism, it would be fruitless speculation to concentrate on the possibilities for human relationships whose time and conditions were not yet ready. The dualism between spirit and matter under capitalism (which had stultified the possibilities of anything more than alienated relationships) would be overcome only in the future "by virtue of the practical energy of man."[39]

It may be also that Marx was reluctant to specify the possibilities of genuine mutual community because of his belief that human beings' needs and possibilities were "elastic" and almost infinitely open.[40] These possibilities included many that were not merely material or economic. Marx condemns capitalism in part because it does not provide time or conditions in which persons can "enjoy [their] personalit[ies], realize [their] natural capacities and *spiritual* [emphasis added] aims."[41] In communism, we need to remember, no one will have an exclusive sphere of activity "but each can become accomplished in any branch he wishes . . . without ever becoming" that which he does.[42] Freedom, in this context, seems to mean opportunity for noncoerced production, which, as Marx suggests in his reflections on Mill, will be intended as much for the development of others as for oneself. This sense of freedom is significantly different from that assumed in the self-determining organic model that Marx employed on other occasions. In a nonalienated state, freedom would not be needed as a protection *from* others; it would be an opportunity to work *for* others.

At this point the vision of Marx and that of Macmurray begin to touch· in complementary models of community. The touch is tentative and incomplete because Marx never entirely freed himself from the organic model that determined so much of his thinking about social issues. But the possibility of a new dialogue between a recovered vision of community in Marx and the view of community articulated by Macmurray now presents itself because of the failure of both liberal individualism and organic totalitarianism to provide satisfactory bases for personal mutuality. Organic models, like atomistic ones, need to be superceded by forms of relationship that reflect the deepest spiritual dimensions of human life while remaining firmly embedded in the material and historical realities of the human and natural order. In the notion of mutual heterocentrism, of agapaic or altruistic love, that Macmurray develops, we can find the foundation for such a conviction.

NOTES

1. John D. Lewis remarked that Macmurray's pieces in *Marxism* made an "intelligent, undogmatic analysis of the bases of dialectical materialism." John D. Lewis, review of *Marxism*, *American Political Science Review* 29 (1935): 710. C. E. M. Joad remarked that Macmurray "has the knack of investing everything he writes with a certain excitement" and has no fault to find in his treatment of Marx. C. E. M. Joad, review of *Marxism*, *Spectator*, March 29, 1935, 537. Reinhold Niebuhr, commenting on Macmurray's contributions to *Christianity and the Social Crisis*, complained that while Macmurray "sometimes oversimplifies, he has a great gift for approaching ultimate and significant problems with a simple approach which is usually, though not

always, as profound as it is simple." Reinhold Niebuhr, review of *Christianity and the Social Crisis* and *Creative Society*, *New York Herald Tribune Books*, June 14, 1936, 18. Niebuhr believed that *Christianity and the Social Crisis* was the "most important volume in its field published in many years." R. H. Tawney, reviewing *Christianity and the Social Revolution*, recommended Macmurray's piece on the early development of Marx's thought as the best place to start. R. H. Tawney, review of *Christianity and the Social Revolution*, *New Statesman and Nation*, November 9, 1935, 682–83. Two of the more critical reviews came from H. J. Laski, who acknowledges the clarity of Macmurray's work but faults him for lacking in-depth analysis of Marx and communism. H. J. Laski, review of *Aspects of Dialectical Materialism*, *New Statesman and Nation*, January 26, 1935, 114–15. In a much longer critique of Macmurray, written a few years later, Elizabeth Lam takes him to task for failing to do justice to the fullness of Marx's thought. Elizabeth Lam, "Does Macmurray Understand Marx?" *Journal of Religion* 20 (1940): 47–65. Lam unfortunately misunderstands most of what Macmurray was saying.

2. Sidney Hook, *From Hegel to Marx* (Ann Arbor: University of Michigan Press, c. 1950), chap. 1, sec. 2, 4.

3. Melvin Rader, *Marx's Interpretation of History* (New York: Oxford University Press, 1979); and Bertell Ollman, *Alienation*, 2nd ed. (Cambridge: Cambridge University Press, 1976).

4. John Macmurray, *Persons in Relation* (New York: Harper and Brothers, 1961), 157.

5. John Macmurray, "The Unity of Modern Problems," *Journal of Philosophical Studies* 4 (1929): 172, 174.

6. Karl Marx, *Grundrisse: Foundations of the Critique of Political Economy* (rough draft), trans. Martin Nicolaus (Harmondsworth, U.K.: Penguin Books, 1973), 278.

7. Rader, *Marx's Interpretation of History*, 76, 59.

8. Karl Marx, *Economic and Philosophic Manuscripts of 1844*, ed. and introd. Dirk J. Struik, trans. Martin Milligan (New York: International Publishers, 1964), 112.

9. Ollman, *Alienation*, 17.

10. Ollman, *Alienation*, 27.

11. Allen W. Wood, *Karl Marx* (London: Routledge and Kegan Paul, 1981), 106.

12. Wood, *Karl Marx*, 104.

13. Wood, *Karl Marx*, 105.

14. Wood, *Karl Marx*, 208.

15. Wood, *Karl Marx*, 208–9.

16. Marx, *Economic and Philosophical Manuscripts*, 137.

17. Marx, *Economic and Philosophical Manuscripts*, 135.

18. Marx, *Economic and Philosophical Manuscripts*, 138.

19. Marx, *Economic and Philosophical Manuscripts*, 181–82.

20. Marx, *Economic and Philosophical Manuscripts*, 140.

21. Marx, *Economic and Philosophical Manuscripts*, 140.

22. Ollman, *Alienation*, 107.

23. Istvan Meszaros, *Marx's Theory of Alienation* (London: Merlin Press, 1970), 185.

24. Eugene Kamenka, *The Ethical Foundations of Marxism* (New York: Praeger, 1962), 98.

25. Marx, *Economic and Philosophical Manuscripts*, 144.

26. Kamenka, *The Ethical Foundations of Marxism*, 97–98.

27. Kamenka, *The Ethical Foundations of Marxism*, 99.

28. Ollman, *Alienation*, 23.

29. The issue of selflessness or giving the "other" primacy in personal relations will be treated more fully later.

30. The notion of "heterocentricity" will be developed later; it plays a crucial role in Macmurray's mature notion of community.

31. In this context, the term might mean nothing more than "society."

32. Marx, *The German Ideology*, ed. and introd. C. J. Arthur (New York: International Publishers, 1970), 83.

33. Karl Marx, "On James Mill," *Karl Marx: Selected Writings*, ed. David McLellan (Oxford: Oxford University Press, 1977), 120.

34. Marx, "On James Mill," 121.

35. Marx, "On James Mill," 122.

36. Marx, "On James Mill," 122.

37. Marx, "On James Mill," 122.

38. Marx, "On James Mill," 122.

39. Marx, *Economic and Philosophical Manuscripts*, 141.

40. Karl Marx, "Results of the Immediate Process of Production," *Karl Marx: Selected Writings*, ed. David McLellan (Oxford: Oxford University Press, 1977), 521.

41. Marx, "On James Mill," 118.

42. Marx, *The German Ideology*, 53.

5

CHRISTIANITY, FASCISM, AND THE CLUE TO HISTORY

One aspect of Macmurray's treatment of communism and Marxism that looks forward to the integration of religion into his larger political philosophy was his understanding of Judaism as the essential contributor to the meaning of Western history. Because he was looking for a religion that was nonidealist, grounded in the historical and material realities of the world, he was attracted to the Jewish roots of Christianity. He claims in *Creative Society* that Judaism is both "religious through and through" and at the same time completely realistic, capable of unifying every aspect of human social life, both individual and corporate.[1] True religion is a commitment to the integration of all aspects of life in *this* world, not in the next. Judaism instantiates the truth (as Macmurray sees it) that the eternal nature of human persons is expressed fully only in community and that, at least in intention, this truth must be universalized to all persons on earth.[2]

For Macmurray, Jesus is a direct heir of the realism and universal thrust of Judaism. Jesus' announcement of the coming of the Kingdom of God articulates his view that human nature is inherently social, fulfilled only in community, and that the complete material conditions for its fulfillment lie in the future. As long as that future is not striven for by concrete human action (political and economic) in the historical conditions that now prevail, human nature will remain unfulfilled. The truth of Judaism (and, when it is true to its Jewish roots, of Christianity) is that when its religion is real, it is "always alive both to the facts of the empirical situation and to a truth which is denied by the facts, and which is, for all that, their eternal essence. . . . It is because human beings behave actually in a way which denies the reality of their own nature that the redemption of human nature is necessary. The Kingdom of Heaven is at once the truth about human nature and

the distant goal of human development."[3] Jesus' teaching about the Kingdom of God, according to Macmurray, exhibits the main features of *theoretical* communism: that is, the unity of theory and practice, the dialectical development of society, the significance of class conflict, and the importance
of economics in the structuring of social life.

The importance of Judaism in developing the notion and reality of the
Kingdom of God is carried further in Macmurray's 1938 book *The Clue to
History*, which offers the tantalizing, and not always successfully defended,
claim that history cannot help but fulfill God's intentions in the long run
because those intentions are built into reality and specifically into human
nature. What is opposed to human nature is ultimately self-defeating. The
Jews have provided the world with a religious consciousness that is profoundly realistic because it understands God's intentions and therefore *integrates* the world and the person into a unified whole: spirit and matter, the
personal and the economic, the individual and society.

Embracing the religious consciousness of Judaism is the clue to history.
To be fully religious is to be fully engaged, through human action, with the
world of which one is a part. The Jews did not *have* a religion: they *were* a
religion. Their God was a worker, an agent engaged with them and their
world in a practical way.[4] That is why they linked love of God so closely to
love of neighbor. This linkage led them to view society as both egalitarian
and democratic, "as a practice of social relation which is totally incompatible with class-distinction, either on an economic or on a caste basis."[5]

The religious concept of the "Fall" is interpreted by Macmurray as
meaning that human beings are not living in accordance with the essential
nature God had given them in creation. Their actual behavior is not a true
expression of their real nature. God works for a historical future in which
the contradiction between human nature as it now is and what it can be has
been overcome. "This means that the reconciliation of ideal and actual is
projected into the future as an actual event in time."[6] This event requires
cooperative action between human beings and God. History becomes the
arena for the working out of God's intention as embedded in created human nature. Thus Hebrew religion is both religious (it sees history in the
light of God's acts and intentions) and empirical (it looks to see what is actually happening in history as the realization of God's intentions). Macmurray reads Hebraic-Christian religion in a decidedly this-worldly, historical
sense.

He sees social failure as a sign of alienation or departure from the will
of God for human beings.[7] It is in and through the historical development
of the social nature of human beings (culminating in the experience of fel-

lowship or mutuality in community) that God's intentions are realized. For Macmurray, the more we know about the principles of social life, the more we understand God's purpose in history. "There is no possibility of distinguishing between the principles which actually determine social success or failure, and the divine law which reveals the will of God for his people. There is no secular law which could be contrasted with a divine law, nor is there any secular thought which could be in conflict with religious thought."[8]

In Macmurray's understanding, Jesus, a Jew, is thoroughly imbued with this "religious" understanding of the inseparability of the empirical from the religious. The clue to understanding Jesus, a prophet in the Jewish tradition, is that for his religious consciousness "a statement about society is a religious statement and a statement about God has an immediate and direct reference to society."[9] Jesus believed that only by cooperating with the divine intention could one achieve the fulfillment of one's own basic intentions for living life in the fullest possible way. Jesus was the historical personage who made it possible for human beings to adopt consciously God's purpose as their purpose because it was already "inherent" in their nature.[10] Jesus' great insight was that human life is ultimately more than organic; it is personal. And if the personal life is the essence of human life, and human life will ultimately be brought to fulfillment through human action in cooperation with God's action, then human life must, inevitably, at some point in the future, be fulfilled. "It is the fundamental postulate of religious rationality that the purpose of God must inevitably be achieved. Thus, the discovery of the essence of humanity is the discovery, not merely of what human life ought to be, but of what human life will be when the work of God in history is complete."[11] And God's work cannot ultimately fail. This is the core principle of Macmurray's understanding of history: "Reality cannot frustrate itself."[12] As free agents persons can, of course, choose an intention for themselves that is not in accord with their essential nature. But when this happens, they cannot help but frustrate themselves. "If [a person] refuses the intention which defines his own nature, and so refuses to be himself, he must necessarily define an intention for himself in opposition to his own nature. This process of self-frustration must inevitably prove self-destructive. It follows that wherever Man rejects the discovery of himself he will be committed to a line of action which is attempting to achieve what cannot be achieved. Every such effort will, in the course of its history, defeat itself. It will be impossible, beyond a certain point, to maintain the intention. Its impossibility will be revealed in the process of attempting to achieve it."[13]

This claim is at the heart of Macmurray's dialectical reading of history. He believes that any personal or social intention that is in conflict with the course of history as intended by God will spawn its opposite, which in the end will produce a synthesis that is more nearly in conformity with reality and thus more likely to succeed. (Macmurray fails, I think, to substantiate this claim, and it is one he draws from Hegel and Marx without extended argument or defense). What has to be understood, however, is that Macmurray was trying to find a rational explanation for why the course of European history will ultimately lead to the defeat of fascism and the triumph of socialism. The religious source that justifies this explanation was his understanding of the Hebrew consciousness that eventually gets carried over into Christianity (when it is being true to itself). In Jesus and the Jews there arises a discovery of a "law of human history" that enables us to see in which direction history is moving if we align our own intentions with those of "reality" (i.e., God's intention).

THE POLITICAL IMPLICATIONS OF RELIGION: THE CASE OF FASCISM

What is the political significance of this theological reflection? For Macmurray it is that any political intention other than one that aims for what God aims for, namely a free and equal humanity able to experience community, must necessarily fail historically. Any movement for freedom and equality in society must ultimately succeed because it is in harmony with the will of God and with the true nature of human being. Under the individualist mode of consciousness (which is opposed to the religious mode embodied in Jesus and the Jews), one hides one's true nature from oneself through a dualistic separation between work and spiritual freedom. But in so doing, the individualist with political and economic power separates himself from the cooperative society of laborers under his control. "In this way there is created an increasing dualism in society between a class of owners who are in practice competing individualists and a class of workers who are in practice co-operating collectively."[14] As a dualism, however, this practice cannot be sustained indefinitely, because it is in opposition to the nature of persons.

In the meantime, however, what is created is fascism, which is built on the belief that what is needed to reconcile the conflicts among individuals is a strong political leader. The intellectual means for creating a better, more egalitarian and free society already existed, but what was lacking was the emotional motive to do it. Because under dualism emotion was subordinated to intellect, the desire to use the means for creating a just society had not been developed or encouraged. Emotion, as Macmurray had argued in *Reason and Emotion*, is the unifying factor in human life.[15] It unifies the individual and social dimensions of the human person. When emotion is suppressed in favor of intellectual superiority, it acts as a "negative force" that opposes the intellect (instead of being unified with it). The impulses of suppressed emotion become anti-egalitarian and anti-progressive.[16] And this is "the simple explanation of the spiritual character of fascism."[17] It leads to a national collectivism that is destructive, not constructive. It seeks to destroy individual freedom, democracy, and equality. Fascism is, paradoxically, both collectivist and individualist (and thus in contradiction with itself). Echoing the themes of organicism, Macmurray understood the fascist state as a "collective individualism," one in which "the opposition of the individual and society is bridged by a 'mystical' identification of the individual with the society to which he belongs." Society becomes the individual's "greater self."[18] The state or the nation becomes a person in itself. And, as an individual, it seeks absolute freedom for itself in relation to other states or nations. This leads to a fear-driven international competition for wealth, which, it is believed, will make the successful competitors free from all the others. The collective individualism of fascism is ultimately self-contradictory and impossible to sustain because no group of persons can be fulfilled as long as it remains in opposition to all other groups of persons.

Within the fascist state, according to Macmurray, an inner contradiction also exists. It must convince its members that they should give themselves completely to the services of the state because they *belong* to the state (as organs belong to the organism of which they are a part). But the more they devote themselves to this mystical ideal of oneness with the state, the more they lose their individual freedoms. This is politically inherently unstable. "The inner problem of fascist society is the necessity of maintaining, with increasing difficulty, the mystical idealism on which it depends. Unless the majority of its members find a symbolic satisfaction in the achievements of the State and its leader, fascism must crumble."[19] To keep this problem from developing, fascism must insist upon the dualism between reason and emotion. The critical faculties of reason must be subordinated to emotion. Emotion must be directed toward the symbols of the state and the leader's ability to manipulate those symbols so that the masses of people will be emotionally satisfied, even if there result no empirical, political, or economic achievements. The emotions that fascism evokes are those that have previously been suppressed by the dualism of mind and matter, and thus manifest themselves in destructive forms. In bringing these emotions to the surface, however, fascism produces its own opposite: a yearning for socialism. What Macmurray meant by this is that fascism is based on a longing for a collective unity. But it can only impose this unity by totalitarian force driven by fear and by the denial of individual freedom and equality. Socialism is the practical, and rational, realization of the hunger for collective unity that enshrines individual freedom and equality (as least as Macmurray understood socialism). And socialism can only be achieved when the anti-intellectual passions that drive fascism run themselves into a destructive dead-end.

In this argument Macmurray relied upon a complex, and not very satisfying, exploitation of a form of dialectical thinking. He assumed that whatever is ultimately false to human nature (such as dualism, idealism, the subordination of reason to passion, or individualism) cannot in the end prevail historically. But prior to the ultimate victory of true human nature, there will be dialectical reversals. The unsuccessful attempt to achieve the opposite of what God intends would lead to the triumph of God's will (which is built into human nature). Focusing on fascism, Macmurray argued that in its dualism it has made the world of the human spirit (freedom, equality) a different world to be enjoyed only in the "next" life and has turned the "real" world into one of destruction, competition, and collective individualism. But as the rational understanding of what is truly good for human nature comes to consciousness, as theory and practice are unified, the spirit world becomes integrated with the real world in an integral, nondualistic whole.

Returning to his religious reading of this process, Macmurray argued that, for a time, Christianity could be relegated to the symbolic spiritual world and used to represent it. This is, however, in contradiction to its true nature, which is grounded in Judaism's unity of theory and practice. When it is being true to its Jewish roots, Christianity cannot be only symbolic, dualist, and idealist. It must work practically for the achievement of a community of persons not divided by nationality, race, or gender. Fascism could accept a Christianity that was otherworldly, spiritualist, and dualist. But it could not accept a Christianity that seeks community through a social, political, and economic reconstruction of current practices that intend democracy, equality, and freedom. Thus fascism will turn against Christianity in its practical form and, in so doing, will be in contradiction with the thrust of history that (since it is God's will) cannot ultimately be frustrated.

Macmurray also had a curious, and easily misunderstood, treatment of the relation between Christianity and Judaism *since the time of Jesus*. While he believed that Jesus fully embodied the Jewish consciousness, he thought

Judaism made a serious mistake in rejecting Jesus and turning instead to what he called a "racialist" understanding of its identity. The Jewish consciousness (the unity of humankind in freedom and equality within the spatio-temporal framework of the real world) turned against itself when it rejected Jesus as the one who had fully embodied that Jewish consciousness. Although Christianity became "the Jewish contribution to the Western tradition,"[20] the Jews of Jesus' time "refused to become consciously the means for the achievement of a universal community in which race was no longer the basis of human relationship. Instead they cling to their racial distinctness and insisted upon their racial superiority. By this refusal of their own reality," they achieved the opposite of their intention. "It is the exclusive racialism of the Jewish people which is their real rejection of the substance of Christianity and by this rejection they are self-isolated from the community of mankind."[21]

This is a highly tendentious reading of Judaism and the Jews, and one which, at first blush, seems to suggest that by cutting themselves off from the deeper meaning of their own Jewish consciousness the Jews had brought upon themselves the calamities inflicted upon them by the Christian West. I do not think this is what Macmurray intended to say, but he did not protect himself very well from this interpretation. Macmurray was, in effect, pitting the "Jewish consciousness" (whose ultimate historical triumph fills him, he declares, "with joyous exhilaration"[22]) against wrong decisions made by the Jewish people in rejecting Jesus as the embodiment of the same consciousness. But such a reading of history fits Macmurray's tendency to employ somewhat casually dialectical categories of thesis, antithesis, and synthesis.

In the end, he argued, the racialism of Judaism since the time of Jesus spawned a rival: the racialism of Nazi Germany. While the Jewish people continued to be unified by religion alone (without a common homeland, leader, or institutionalized economic and political organizations), Nazism took over the Jewish claim to the superiority of race. The Jews, according to Macmurray, are living witness to the reality of a social unity that does not depend upon statehood, nationality, organization, or leadership.[23] In this respect, they point to a universal community of persons that will also transcend the trappings of nationhood and collective individualism. They stand as a direct threat to the consciousness of Germany under Hitler: they point beyond the glorification of the state or race. Macmurray said that "the only real community in which the Jewish problem could be solved would be the community of humanity in which race was no longer a principle of unity."[24]

Racialism, however, is ultimately not sustainable as a basis for real human community. It is a passion, an "eruption of the unconscious which defies rational control."[25] And in the end, it cannot work in practice. It creates artificial barriers and boundaries in the identities of persons that cannot be sustained if genuine communities of equality, democracy, trust, and love are to be established. Jewish consciousness must be rescued from its negative expression in racialism and restored to its universalistic vision of a human community built on the principles of inclusive love and justice. Christianity, he believed, "negates the negation" and brings into being what fascism opposes, namely "the socialist commonwealth of the world. The fundamental law of human nature cannot be broken. . . . The will to power is self-frustrating."[26]

There is clearly an audaciousness in Macmurray's reading of history, and in particular of the relation between Judaism and Christianity. He wrote in a way that was not sensitive to the particularities, ambiguities, nuances, and contingencies of Western European history. He applied a too abstract architectonic to the course of historical and religious events to carry much conviction. Even his claims for Christianity were clearly outside the mainstream.

Reinhold Niebuhr's review of *The Clue to History* took Macmurray to task precisely for his utopianism, a misunderstanding of human sin (which constantly tempts persons to deny their essential nature), and a failure to appreciate the significance of the Cross, which casts in doubt any optimistic reading of the direction of human history.[27] Whether Macmurray was truly the naive utopian thinker this critique claimed is something to be taken up more fully later. What certainly can be admired in Macmurray's work was his attempt to find a "clue" to history that would reconcile the yearnings people feel for a more authentic, fulfilled human life and the historical conditions with which they have to deal in seeking to fulfill those yearnings. What Macmurray forces us to do is to take seriously (increasingly difficult in a postmodern, deconstructive age) the possibility that there really is a clue to history, a meaning behind what otherwise might appear to be the random concatenation of meaningless events following each other in a petty pace from day to day. Whether he was right in believing that there is a unifying intention that can weave together the material conditions of the world and the human desire to find fulfillment in personal relations is another question.

RELIGION, POLITICS AND SOCIETY: MACMURRAY IN THE LATE 1930s

In the latter half of the 1930s, Macmurray's interest in communism and socialism did not fade but his attention was also directed somewhat more fully toward the role of religion, especially Christianity, in the development of a more just and democratic society. He was also a keen observer of political movements taking place in Great Britain, Russia, and Germany. His written work took three forms during this period: formal monographs (e.g., *The Structure of Religious Experience*, 1936), occasional informal pieces for "the Christian Left," and unpublished lectures (carefully recorded by those present) to various audiences in the United Kingdom and Canada. During this period no really new ground was broken, but old themes were revisited and reflections on contemporary issues were common.

In 1936 Macmurray addressed specifically the role of religion in the modern world and, in particular, its role in the development of community. One work, based on the Terry Lectures given at Yale University in April of that year, was *The Structure of Religious Experience*.[28] The other work devoted to religion was *Religion in the Modern World*, the notes taken from talks Macmurray gave to the Student Christian Movement in Ontario (presumably on the same trip that had taken him to Yale in April).[29]

His religious views were characterized by an emphasis on the practical, empirical expression of religion in the "real" world. Religion, he argued in *The Structure of Religious Experience*, should be progressive and empirically based. As empirical, religion should be grounded upon "facts," upon "tying the inner activities of the mind tightly, at both ends, to the immediate realities of universal human experience."[30] He compares religion, as a form of valuation or attitude of mind, to science and art. Knowing something in order to use it for a purpose is scientific; knowing something for its intrinsic value is art; and religion is the reconciliation of valuing things both for utility and for intrinsic worth. In particular we value persons both in themselves and in their relation to us. "The religious attitude sets the relationship of the self to other selves at the center of valuation and values everything else in relation to this. For such an attitude the main business of life consists in understanding, appreciating, and creating the full reality of personal relationship. The task of religion is the realization of fellowship. The religious activity of the self is its effort to enter into communion with the Other."[31] But this effort must be consciously and persistently *intentional*. By intending relationship with others, one is doing more than acknowledging the *fact* of relationship. Intentionality as the guide to ongoing human action is the uniquely human characteristic. Personal relationships "must, moreover, be mutually affirmed and mutually chosen."[32] Religion is about the restoration of relationality, about the reconciliation of persons following their rupture with God and other persons. Throughout the process of reconciliation, moreover, all parties must have their freedom as agents affirmed.

This will involve an increase in the inclusiveness of community and a deepening of the intensity of communion.[33] The broadening of a group's membership is facilitated by social cooperation and the political means for its development and maintenance. "Other things being equal, the larger the group is, the more effective and productive co-operation becomes."[34] But "effective" and "productive" cooperation do not constitute the heart of a community of personal relationships. A cooperation that is "motived purely by its profitableness to the persons concerned, but which includes no intention of personal relation" is not a community. "In such cases we find that a society of actual relationships is set up, but it is not supported by any consciousness of community."[35]

Such a society may remain stable as long as it is not under extraordinary stress. If the stress becomes too much, the society will collapse "unless it can be sustained by a personal loyalty."[36] A society can maintain itself even when the relations that constitute it are unconscious (controlled by the mechanisms of the state). But when they become conscious, they must be affirmed as personal relations or else repudiated.[37] In other words, cooperative society by itself will prove to be insufficient for fulfilling the development of persons as persons. Persons must intend either a universal community or retreat into smaller societies built around fear and hatred of other societies. "Community refused means hatred, opposition, and war."[38]

Macmurray pointed out that, at the international level, a "network of economic co-operation which crossed national boundaries . . . [had become] almost world-wide."[39] This had not meant an automatic embrace of the intention for universal community. According to Macmurray, that failure meant "we must restrict co-operation once more within the limits of the existing communities [I think he meant "societies"], while remaining conscious of the possibility which we are refusing. In that case, the refusal becomes a gesture of hostility and leads inevitably in the direction of active hostility and war."[40] In these comments Macmurray was suggesting, once again, the something more than shared political principles that was needed to sustain unity. That "more" is community as something over and above but containing elements of society. It is almost as if Macmurray had unconsciously adopted a modified version of Hegel's *aufhebung*, the taking up into itself of a phase of development that is abrogated, annulled, done away with, but also preserved and superceded in the dialectical process.[41] Community abrogates and annuls society (in the sense of not regarding it as the final and complete form of personal relationship) but also preserves it in the sense of subordinating its structures to the development of friendship, and supercedes it in the sense that it takes the form of relationship (the personal or superorganic) to a higher level more in keeping with the full potentiality of the human person as created by God. This suggests a dynamic and complex relationship between society and community that will be much more fully worked out in the Gifford Lectures of the mid-1950s. What is clear at this stage of his intellectual biography is that Macmurray could not let go of either the political/economic dimensions of human life (society) nor of another form of human relationship (community) that goes beyond them. Religious reflection "reveals the possibility of a universal community of mankind, of a perfectly harmonious co-operation of all men irrespective of differences, in a spirit of universal brotherhood."[42] The task for religious action was, Macmurray conceded (tempering the utopianism of the former statement), staggering in light of the "tragic immensity of the task set for it." Nevertheless if religion is going to avoid dualism and unite theory and practice, it must adopt the intention not just of fellowship but of the crucial empirical precondition for it, "the actuality of economic interdependence."[43]

The lecture series entitled "Religion in the Modern World," which Macmurray gave to students in Ontario in 1936, continued the theme of linking religion to economic and political issues. He argued that as a result of the First World War, the world was moving away from individualism and becoming increasingly socialized,[44] which included a movement from economic anarchy to economic order. He also claimed that the knowledge of politics and economics needed for a just society was already available but what was lacking was the "reconciliation of human wills," and that is the task of religion.[45] Until that task is completed, society must be "integrated" by principles of justice, equity, and democracy.[46] Economic justice may not be the supremely important thing in human life, but it is like the health of the body. "If the economic organization falls sick, then nothing else is important *for the time*. No real human social life is possible till the economic organization is restored to health. We must recognize that the economic system is making the personal life possible."[47]

Specifically, he argued that any just economic policy must be developed on the basis of class consciousness. There are, he asserts, two societies: the working class and the capitalist class, and no single economic policy can fit them both. For him it was clear that "the future of the Kingdom of Heaven depends on the working class taking over control."[48] Like Marx he believed that the whole economic order rests on labor because it alone transforms the world into what is useful to human beings. The problem is to eliminate the difference between the social process by which labor produces and the individual ownership of that process by the capitalists.

THE ISSUES OF SEXUAL RELATIONS
AND SOCIAL PLANNING

In the talks that formed *Religion in the Modern World*, Macmurray addressed the question of the equality of the sexes. As in the talks that were the basis of *Reason and Emotion*, Macmurray lamented the dualism that infects the relations between men and women. As long as those relationships are conceived primarily in functional or organic terms, and as long as men control the concepts that determine those relationships, the equality of the sexes will be impossible. Men have "increased and intensified the functional distinction between the sexes.... Women have been left to preserve other bonds, to concentrate on the emotional, unifying activity."[49] The realm of emotion has been left to women and, as a completely unintended result, men have been left emotionally impoverished (or as he says elsewhere "unreal") because they fail to emotionally appreciate the value of what is other than themselves.[50] But women are more and more demanding their own individual rights and freedoms. And as this happens, the unity of society, built on the functional distinctions determined by men, begins to break down. If social unity is to be restored, it can only be by gender equality. "We must find a way in which men can learn the necessary expertness in the emotional field and women in the technical field."[51] Equality and freedom are integral to human relations and are not based on gender roles. As long as the inequality between men and women is enshrined in law and economic structures, as they are in capitalism, husband and wife cannot be free and equal. (Macmurray thought, somewhat naively, that this equality had begun to be real in Russia.)[52]

The theme in these two sets of lectures of linking religious intention with economic/political issues carried over into Macmurray's more occasional pieces written for what was called the Auxiliary Movement of the Christian Left during the latter half of the 1930s. Beginning in 1937 and working closely with economic thinker and friend Karl Polanyi, Macmurray was a major contributor to its newsletters. Most of his applied political analysis is found within those pages. At the same time, the principle behind the newsletters was the attempt to make Christianity a central contributor to the historical process of developing a humane society and a personal community. The Auxiliary Movement began, according to Macmurray, with the discovery that religion and politics must not be kept separate[53] and that Christianity must consciously recognize the nature of the process that was leading to a "socialist community founded on the communal ownership of the means of production" and its role in that process.[54] This, he argued should be the political task of the Christian Left.

Politics must become "part of that creative activity in which we are all continuously involved with God, whether we like it or not, for the transformation of human relationships and the establishment of the kingdom of Heaven on earth." Addressing political and economic transformation demands attention because political and economic relationships are "at once part, and the material basis of, the structure of personal life."[55] Even more strongly he asserts that "the economic and political relations of men are not merely the basis of personal life, they are an inherent part of it *and the criterion of its reality*."[56] Macmurray was convinced that the personal life of community, toward which Christianity should be moving people, is not possible without a total transformation of the "existing political and economic structure of human life as a whole."[57] At the same time religion's essential task "involves a practical effort to transform the structure of the secular world and [in this sense] . . . politics really is religious whether people deny it or not."[58] However, to the extent that the organized church continues to maintain the distinction between religion and secular life, organized religion is an obstacle to progress. By withdrawing religion from the world, the Church "forces the State to undertake the religious task of the unification of the inner life of society,"[59] a task for which it is profoundly unsuited. Religion ought to be the vehicle for creating community because people, Macmurray asserted, can only be loved, not coerced, into community.

Not surprisingly, much of the political focus of the Christian Left was on the dangers of fascism and the potential of communism in the Soviet Union to instantiate the political goals of socialism. Speaking for the Christian Left, Macmurray said that socialism was the "positive movement of the world in the Christian direction."[60] It meant the abolition of private ownership of the means of production and its replacement by production for use, not profit. The Christian Left also called for the abolition of political and racial domination and, somewhat vaguely, the creation of a universal commonwealth of peoples.

One issue the Christian Left faced without hesitation was what stance to take toward the Soviet Union. Macmurray had said in 1935 that "the new society that is growing up in Russia looks more like the fulfillment of the promises [originally articulated by Christianity] than anything the world has seen, and it certainly holds the key to our future."[61] Nevertheless he repeated his view, expressed earlier as well in his work on Marx and the philosophy of communism, that Christianity and communism (which in practice meant the Soviet Union) cannot, in principle, be allies, since the latter systematically denies the importance of religion and in so doing is embarked on not just a mistaken venture but one that is "suicidal."[62] Communism is

not the real opposite to fascism: only democracy is the alternative to the latter. This means that the Christian Left would not support everything the
Soviet Union was doing but it did recognize that a "socialist economy" had
emerged in Russia.[63] At the same time, Macmurray argued, it is important
to acknowledge that the limitations of socialism in the Soviet Union are due
to its failure to understand the true nature of religion "and this prevents the
development of Socialist society in Russia and partly accounts for the strength
of Fascism in the rest of the world."[64]

By the early 1940s Macmurray had become increasingly critical of
the Soviet experiment. With both Russia's alliance with Germany and its
invasion of Finland as background, and in line with his earlier conviction
(in *The Clue to History*) that fascism and bolshevism were "dialectical opposites," Macmurray attacked Russia for having implicitly "revealed a
praxis of a peculiarly Hitlerian type, based on trickery and violence. The
type of action which now flows from Russian social life is totally at vari-
ance with the position of the Christian Left. A Christian socialism would
dictate and effect a quite different policy and praxis."[65] He called for a
condemnation of Russia and Stalin "without equivocation." Socialism,
which of course he still supported, could only be achieved through a democratic and economic ordering of social life. He called for a repudiation
of the "Marxist" position (while incorporating elements of "marxism"
into the Left's position), as long as the former is unable to understand and
use the religious ground on which alone true human community can be
established. "So long as Russia remains intolerant of religion large num-
bers of folks . . . must find it impossible to believe that she is democratic,
on the true line of progress."[66] No matter how valuable the material ad-
vances in Russia have been for its people, true democrats must wonder
whether "the material benefits of socialism [in Russia] may not have to be
bought at the price of that freedom of the spirit which alone could make
them worth possessing."[67]

Although his writings for the Christian Left would continue into the
early 1940s, one of Macmurray's last political analyses written in the 1930s,
"Valuations in Fascist and Communist States," was indicative of his growing
interest in finding a scientific basis for his political and economic arguments.[68] (He would publish in the final year of that decade his only major
book devoted exclusively to science, appropriately entitled *The Boundaries of
Science*.[69]) In "Valuations" Macmurray took up the issue of social planning
as it is carried out with the help of the science of sociology. Social planning,
he insisted, cannot exist without a prior conscious valuing of social life as a
whole. At one level, the scientist can infer the values of a given society by

observing its behaviors. At another level, however, values can only be expressed by the agents who are doing the valuing. And there is often a split between these two levels of value. "There is a notable discordance, in social behaviour, between the principles of valuation which actually enter into the determination of behaviour, and the expression of these principles by the persons concerned."[70] This discrepancy is the disagreement of theory with practice, the unity of which Macmurray has been at pains to restore. This disagreement reflects a distinction between what Macmurray called a "real" valuation and an "ideal" valuation. The former guides intentional action. The latter does not envision any activities that would be necessary to realize it.[71] The problem with capitalist societies is that they labor under ideal valuations, wherein the greatest degree of divergence between theory and practice occurs.

The ideal values are freedom, equality, humanity, and progress.[72] These ideal values, however, are not instantiated in the capitalist world: they are subverted so that individualism, not freedom, equality, or humanity, prevails. Because the perversion of these values encourages a struggle for individual power, exploitation of the weak and social inequality are the "real" values of the society. As long as the gap between the real and ideal values is hidden from consciousness, the society can superficially maintain both sets of values, no matter how at odds with each other they are. If conscious social planning takes place, however, the discrepancies between the values will appear and the dualism of ideal and practical valuation will be challenged. At this point, the society must choose which values will guide its social planning and the structures of the society made to conform to them. A planned society is one that requires a "conscious co-operation for a defined social purpose."[73] If that cooperation is among the members of the working class, then the social planning will take a communist form. Under fascism, planning is done within an organic hierarchy driven by the fear of communism, and thus fascism is unable to project a positive ideal or purpose for the society. It becomes anti-democratic, anti-socialist, and anti-progressive.

In short, genuine scientific planning ought to be subordinate to an overarching purpose based on the intent to close the gap between real and ideal values. Because Macmurray believed that genuine science cannot, in the end, be untrue to the reality that God has created, it must reflect the material, political, and economic infrastructures that will advance the possibility of community. Thus there need be no conflict between religion (the agent of community) and science (the means for discovering the realities that religion must utilize in carrying out its agency).

CONSTRUCTIVE DEMOCRACY

Events in the Soviet Union and the declining fortunes of the Christian Left in Great Britain led Macmurray in the 1940s to address more fully the contours and elements of the kind of democratic socialism at home he had been urging for the past decade.[74] In a run-up to his most fully worked out analysis of a democratic society (*Constructive Democracy*), Macmurray wrote a number of crucial pieces for the Christian Left beginning in March 1940 that discussed the relation between socialism, democracy, totalitarianism, and Marxism. In some of these he makes significant modifications in positions he had taken in the 1930s.

Having indicated his severe disappointment and anger at Russia's invasion of Finland, Macmurray saw a major divide opening up between Marxist societies and Christian democratic socialism. The meaning of democratic socialism, he repeated, is religious, not just political (though it is also political).[75] If democracy is the expression of individual human freedom (which is essential to the nature of persons), then the state can only be a means to an end (i.e., community). For the totalitarian, whether fascist or communist, the state is an end in itself that its citizens are to serve. For the democrat the state's political authority must be limited.

The task of democratic government, therefore, is to determine the proper limits of political authority and to create the organizations (the "effective machinery") that will allow it to do its job efficiently and within its proper limits. One part of its task, which has been lacking in capitalist democracies, is bringing the economic order under the control of political authority.[76] At the same time, the cultural life of community must be preserved free of political control. Cultural life requires a socialist economy as its substructure but must thrive on its own terms, not those dictated by the political and economic forces of society. The personal values that constitute the deepest forms of personal life are beyond the control of the state. Marx believed that a socialist society would, by virtue of its economic structure, necessarily produce an intrinsically valuable cultural superstructure.[77] Marx, however, was still stuck in an organic model of social life and thus failed to see the superorganic dimension of human life.

Macmurray does not dismiss the organic structuring of economic relations provided that they do not determine or subsume the full life of the persons who participate in them. "The organized society of economic functions is a means to the personal life of men in Community. This is what the organic view (and the Totalitarianism it implies and in the end creates) denies. It is what democracy affirms."[78]

As long as society has no place for genuine community, efficiency will be the dominant value. Efficiency, however, is an organic value. As such it has no moral worth. In an organic society, the will to power and the need to survive and dominate others become the ends for which the members strive. The human purpose behind efficiency (and the social organizations it creates and utilizes) is lost.

These remarks lay down the markers for Macmurray's more extensive analysis of government, the state, and community. In December 1942, he gave two lectures at University College, London, that were published as *Constructive Democracy*.[79] It was his most well-worked-out attempt at political philosophy prior to the Gifford Lectures over a decade later. Using Hegelian phraseology, Macmurray opened the lectures by arguing that "we" (the Western European societies) were moving from negative government to positive government. He wanted his comments to provide a democratic solution to the problems involved in this transition, especially those caused by the First World War and what he believed would be its victorious aftermath.[80] In his first lecture, "The Liberal Tradition and Negative Democracy," Macmurray reprised the history of English democracy. He argued that it had two aspects: the cultural and the economic. In the cultural sphere, the struggle for and achievement of religious freedom was its cardinal accomplishment and was the basis for other cultural developments and the core of democracy. In the economic sphere, the struggle for free trade had been paramount.

Macmurray defined democracy as the "denial of the omnicompetence of government." He argued that by limiting government's power to the nonreligious sphere, the attainment of religious freedom reveals the limits of politics and the state.[81] At the same time it implies the freedom of all cultural activities from interference by the state.

In the economic sphere, free trade was of particular benefit to the "men who controlled capital investment, and who needed, among other things, to obtain control of labour."[82] This control was not, of course, of equal interest to the working class. The liberal tradition, in Macmurray's reading of it, sided with the owners of capital, and one of the signal achievements of that tradition was the enshrining of the inviolable right to private property. Consequently, for negative democracy, complete freedom was to be given to economic interests (which rest on private property) and government was to withdraw itself from interference in or oversight of them. This view "denies to government the power to use the economic resources of the community [presumably Macmurray meant "society"] for the benefit of the community."[83] Nevertheless, economic freedom without government interference or control was an ideal, never fully reachable in practice. Industrialization had led to a constriction of economic freedom as the conflict between labor and capital grew and they both looked to government to resolve their differences. Despite the failure to achieve complete economic freedom, wealth has been concentrated more and more in the hands of an oligarchy.[84] Political oversight of economic initiative has been kept to a bare minimum except in extreme cases where the very security of the society itself was at stake or the welfare of the people was "grossly interfered with" by the economic privileges of the oligarchy.[85] Nevertheless, the power of the economic oligarchy winds up determining much of cultural life precisely because it has a concentration of power.

The move to what Macmurray called "positive" government comes when people give to the government the right to exercise a "positive control of the material life of its citizens, if it determines what use shall be made of the material resources of the nation, decides what shall be produced and how much of each product, and determines directly the organization of production and distribution in industry and the regulation and allotment of financial resources."[86] This is as clear a statement by Macmurray that one can find as to what socialism is in practice. Unfortunately, he conceded, positive government is also associated in both Germany and Russia with the state's attempt to control the cultural as well as the economic life of its citizens and thus produces the denial of democracy in all spheres.

Macmurray wanted to argue that democracy need not be wedded to a rejection of the particular forms of positive government found in fascism and communism. It is possible, he argued, for there to be restrictions on economic liberty without corresponding restrictions on cultural freedom. Nevertheless, there must be an economic sphere underlying the cultural one. In a claim that anticipates the contemporary liberalism of John Rawls, Macmurray said that "the economic activities of a community [society] are the indispensable basis for its cultural life. The means of life are also the means of a good life. The purpose of democracy in limiting the authority of government is to set free the personal and cultural life of the community and its members; and the necessity for this lies in the fact that freedom is the life blood of all culture and the condition of the good life."[87]

In the second of the two lectures, "The Problem of Positive Government," Macmurray took up the issue of how, given the virtue of controlling economic activity and resources by government, the latter can still be kept within bounds so as not to intrude itself into the cultural and personal freedoms necessary for the full development of the individual person-in-community. Positive government must be linked with positive, or constructive, democracy. The problem is to maintain the vitality of democracy while giving to government authority in the "material" field, that is, in the economic life of the society. In negative democracy this authority is in the hands of private individuals who own the economic resources as their private property. This ownership, limited to a relatively small number of oligarchs, is a fundamental threat to democracy. Their views and power will have a disproportionate influence on the development of public policy. When power to control the economic life of the nation shifts to positive government, the people as a whole will have the responsibility to plan and administer the economy. Macmurray believes this responsibility does not eliminate the need to delegate some of the economic work to private individuals and groups, provided that they remain subject to public supervision and regulation.[88] Curiously Macmurray did not actually call for such a positive government (though it is abundantly clear that he favored such a move). Instead, he said he was mainly concerned with pointing out the dangers in a move to positive government.

As the transition to positive government occurs, the major political players will likely be, at first, the economic players who had disproportionate influence under negative government. Their habits of control would not easily be changed into the habits necessary for a society that is fully democratic. They are by habit given to autocratic control of whatever is under their authority. Thus one of the first tasks during the transition must be to establish a "new instrument of effective public control" of the economic functions that will, in part, utilize the talents of those who previously ran the economic machinery under negative government.[89]

Macmurray believed that the system of economic practice under capitalism, by the early 1940s in Great Britain, had made it almost inevitable that concentration of economic power would occur. An economic system made up of small private enterprises (as Adam Smith envisioned capitalism) was no longer viable. Government was already having to intervene in the economic order to regulate relations between capital and labor and the process of trade with other nations. Monopolies were becoming more frequent and could only be controlled by the power of government. Unemployment on the kind of scale nations were facing required government intervention. For Macmurray this meant that a "controlled economy" was increasingly viable, and he pointed out that such control had helped Britain make it through the war.

So the real question for him was what were the conditions necessary to enable government to administer the economy without having it intrude into the arena of cultural, spiritual, and moral life. The answer could only be a vital democracy that would both determine and oversee the economy and be prepared to limit the authority of government in areas where it should not venture. One great resource for doing this would be "the democratic inventiveness of the people and the sagacity of democratic statesmen."[90]

Second, the people, through democratic deliberation and participation, must answer the question "how are the rights of man to be maintained against the claims of a political system armed with full economic control?"[91] Part of the answer to this question is the ability of the people "to maintain in full vigour, throughout every section of the community, the living spirit of democracy." But democracy is not just a political organization. It is also a "quality" of life, including "a passion for freedom," a "sense of human dignity and personal responsibility," as well as "the love of the fellowship of equals."[92]

Macmurray believed that the traditions of the British people gave hope that these conditions for a constructive democracy within a positive government would be met. These traditions are the spiritual habits of a common democratic life in which such principles as the individual's freedom from tyranny and political control are sacrosanct. The tradition of democracy is powerful enough, he believed, to lead the British people to take the necessary steps to democratize their economic system. But institutional change alone was not sufficient, since people have a tendency to expect more from institutions than they can deliver. Instead, leadership must be imbued with the cultural, moral, and religious sympathies and sentiments to make democracy work. This would require a commitment to public life, and an extension of the civil service that was thoroughly at one with the people in their struggle for a fuller human life. It would also mean, he believed, the retention and deepening of local self-government. The people must help to form, develop, control, and "own" the general economic plan that would then be given to the government to administer. This would require a "lively, positive, and effective participation in self-government by the citizen body."[93] He concluded with the hopeful claim that victory in this effort was likely. "We have every warrant to believe that we can triumph over all the difficulties, and that we shall create that constructive democracy which will make the riches of the earth the full heritage of all her children."[94]

This was a very bracing vision of democratic life in Britain after the war. It was possibly naive and utopian. It certainly required a degree of commitment on the part of the citizenry to full democratic participation in the deliberation, formulation, and execution of the economic and political machinery needed to provide the material substructure on which the cultural, moral life of the nation rested. While religion would, he hoped, play the major role in the determination of that cultural life, politics and economics, formed and regulated by democratic participation, would play the major role in developing its material substructure.

THE CONDITIONS OF PERSONAL FREEDOM

In keeping with one of the essential ingredients in a vital constructive democracy, it is not surprising that one issue Macmurray developed at much greater length in the 1940s was that of individual freedom. The decade opened with his article "Freedom in the Personal Nexus"[95] and concluded in 1949 with a book-length treatment called *Conditions of Freedom.*[96] The theme of *The Clue to History* was repeated in both of these. He argued that freedom is always contextual. We increase or diminish our freedom by changing the conditions within which we act. We experience the lack of freedom when our actions are frustrated. The issue therefore is not metaphysical (are we free?) but practical (how free are we?).

Our fundamental experience of the lack of freedom arises when we believe that other persons are responsible for limiting it. Thus the struggle for freedom is always a struggle against what we take to be oppression by others. And this leads us back to the source of the problem, namely a malfunction in our relationship with other persons. Merely increasing our power will not resolve the problem of freedom, unless there is a change in the nexus of personal relationships.[97]

At the level of society, the solution to the problem of freedom is to remove all forms of tyranny and oppression by altering the organization of societal relationships. This will require using the powers and structures of society to get rid of poverty. But merely achieving this goal does not solve the basic problem of freedom. For in solving it, a society has the tendency to do so by "the organization of tyranny in the totalitarian State."[98] The only way to oppose this totalitarian tendency is through the power of a relationship more basic than that of society: that is, through community. "Freedom can only be maintained in the nexus of human relationship by maintaining the primacy of the personal nexus of community over the functional nexus of organized society."[99] The state must be kept morally subordinate to the community.

The key to the achievement of both communal and societal freedom is the development of equality. In the communal form of relationship, equality is absolutely basic. What can threaten such equality is the will to dominating power. "Where one man seeks power over others, where one class or nation seeks dominion over others, the denial of equality involved creates constraint and limits freedom. And there is no way in which freedom can be restored or increased except by overcoming the desire for power."[100] But how can this be done? Only by confronting the motive that leads to the desire for power: fear of others. And, in the last analysis, fear can only be dealt with by religion and the establishment of community in which fear becomes a "negative" superceded or overcome by the "positive" motive of love. (This argument will be taken up more fully shortly.)

Macmurray's one link to a real political movement was his contribution to Sir Richard Acland's Common Wealth Party in the early 1940s. Common Wealth (or C.W. as it was known) was brought into being in 1942 through a merger of the 1941 Committee (headed by J. B. Priestly) and Acland's Forward March Movement. Acland had been directly influenced by Macmurray and quoted him extensively in his publications setting forth the Common Wealth principles. C.W. was committed to democratic socialism. It pushed for common ownership of the means of production in order to "release the full possibilities of human nature" through cooperative labor.[101] While disclaiming any official affiliation with Christianity, it was clear that Common Wealth was deeply influenced by what it took to be some of its basic values. In 1939 Acland, calling himself a "convert to a thorough-going Socialism based on Christianity," called for a "programme of immediate socialism, based on a thoroughgoing attempt to apply the principles of Christianity to the contemporary world." Macmurray must have played a key role in formulating these principles for the party, since Acland quotes his work, especially "Through Chaos to Community," in which Macmurray claimed that European civilization was the creation of Christianity, and *The Clue to History*, where Macmurray asserted that the direction of history is in accordance with God's will.[102] The party was committed to what it called "vital democracy" and world unity (both of which topics Macmurray either had already addressed or would address soon after). The Labour Party was not appreciative of C.W., which threatened to drain off its far left members. But the threat never materialized; C.W. won only a few by-elections (though Acland was elected to Parliament). With the smashing victory of Labour in the 1945 elections, C.W. ceased to have any influence on British working-class politics.[103]

In 1944 Macmurray left the University of London on invitation to become professor of moral philosophy at the University of Edinburgh (where he would remain until his retirement in 1958). At the end of the decade, he returned to some of the themes in his 1940 article on freedom. If there was any question of his opposition to totalitarianism and to the organic sub-sumption of individuals within a hierarchical organic whole, it is put definitively to rest in this treatment of human freedom.

In 1949 in *Conditions of Freedom*, Macmurray took up again the theme of the need to protect individual freedom from "an intoxication with power, and an unmeasured faith in organization."[104] Even more emphatically than in his earlier work, he asserted that freedom is the "defining character" of the human person. It is the capacity to exercise the uniquely human characteristic of acting with intentionality.[105] The paradox of freedom is that we can choose to act in ways that are in opposition to our own fundamental nature or in opposition to the intentions of others. We can escape from freedom or embrace freedom as the "expression of our own reality. If we use our freedom to escape from freedom we frustrate ourselves."[106] It is only when we choose freely to live in community with others that we act freely and regain our true selves. We know this is true at the societal level because it is only by cooperation with others that the mechanisms of society function smoothly. Short of the experience of community in which freedom is enjoyed fully, freedom is best achieved through justice implemented through a society in which people will cooperate for common ends according to principles of fairness.[107] The state emerges as the one instrument, agreed upon by all, that can use force legitimately to secure political freedom for all its members.

INTERNATIONAL SOCIETY AND JUSTICE

Coming out of the Second World War, Macmurray believed that the world was in the stages of a global revolution whose goal was the unification of the world in a common life. What lies ahead for the struggle for political freedom is the need to adjust the law to meet the needs of all social classes in the search for "essential justice."[108] These needs, he argued, have now become universal in scope. The world wars have brought home the truth that the world is a universal society. Macmurray reaffirmed his "trust in common humanity, which is the working center of any democratic faith."[109] The immediate problem is that although the eyes of the world have been opened to the possibility of a universal society (there is no class or group of people anywhere who are not tied in some fundamental economic or social way to all the rest), there is as yet no effective instrument of justice for such a society. And, short of community, there can be no justice without an international set of laws to compel obedience. The broader the society to which one belongs, the more one must depend upon a "system of law which automatically adjusts the effects of my activities so that no injustice arises anywhere" in the world.[110] Macmurray's chief example of the kind of practical activity that binds the peoples of the world together was economic transaction. He talked of buying a shirt that may, in its production, have been the result of the exploitation of Egyptian workers who grew the cotton. In the world as it was then, however, the furthest that law could reach was the border of the nation-state.[111]

This treatment of constructive democracy and the political implications of personal relationships still begs many questions about Macmurray's treatment of the relation between society and community. They will not be answered until Macmurray devotes himself more thoroughly to the elaboration of what he means by community in relation to society, and this still waits for the Gifford Lectures of 1953–1954.

NOTES

1. John Macmurray, *Creative Society: A Study of the Relation of Christianity to Communism* (London: SCM Press, 1935), 59–60.

2. Macmurray, *Creative Society*, 139.

3. Macmurray, *Creative Society*, 69. The notion of the "essence" of human nature should not be understood to refer to some unchanging "substance" that is beyond the conditions of finite existence. In Macmurray, the term "essence" does not have a well-developed meaning. Generally, it is used simply to refer to something that constitutes the uniquely personal and distinguishes it from the nonpersonal. As he will later argue more completely, if the prime characteristic of human beings is their *agency*, then as agents they can change the conditions (up to a point) under which they live and express their personal essence.

4. There is a great deal of ambiguity in Macmurray's treatment of the concept of God. He often talks about God as "an" agent but there are also frequent references to God as the symbolic referent of the unity of humankind. God's actions sometimes seem to be discrete acts in history; at other times Macmurray writes as if all of history is a single act of God. This is not the place to sort out these problems. But see my book *Together Bound: God, History, and the Religious Community* (New York: Oxford University Press, 1994) for a fuller working out of this issue.

5. John Macmurray, *The Clue to History* (London: SCM Press, 1938), 34.

6. Macmurray, *The Clue to History*, 37.

7. Macmurray, *The Clue to History*, 39.

8. Macmurray, *The Clue to History*, 39.

9. Macmurray, *The Clue to History*, 44.

10. Macmurray, *The Clue to History*, 55.

11. Macmurray, *The Clue to History*, 58.

12. Macmurray, *The Clue to History*, 58. In the light of recent conceptions of God, such as those in process theology, that limit God's power to achieve God's intentions (because of the inherent limitations of a finite world and the counter-intentions of human beings), Macmurray's claims would need much greater refinement than they receive in his own writings. For an attempt to do that, see my *Together Bound: God, History, and The Religious Community*.

13. Macmurray, *The Clue to History*, 59.

14. Macmurray, *The Clue to History*, 199.

15. John Macmurray, *Reason and Emotion* (New York: Barnes and Noble, 1962), 77.

16. Macmurray, *The Clue to History*, 213.

17. Macmurray, *The Clue to History*, 213.

18. Macmurray, *The Clue to History*, 215.

19. Macmurray, *The Clue to History*, 222.

20. Macmurray, *The Clue to History*, 228.

21. Macmurray, *The Clue to History*, 231–32.

22. Macmurray, *The Clue to History*, 227.

23. This was written before the establishment of the state of Israel and without, in my opinion, sufficient attention to the importance of the material dimension of land in Jewish thought (somewhat in contradiction to Macmurray's own high evaluation of the material conditions necessary for the full human life).

24. Macmurray, *The Clue to History*, 230.

25. Macmurray, *The Clue to History*, 234.

26. Macmurray, *The Clue to History*, 237.

27. Reinhold Niebuhr, review of *The Clue to History*, in *Modern Churchman* 29 (May 1939): 75–81.

28. John Macmurray, *The Structure of Religious Experience* (London: Faber and Faber, 1936).

29. Published as *Religion in the Modern World* (Montreal. Associated Literature Service, 1936). Macmurray had given permission for these notes to be published for a limited audience.

30. Macmurray, *The Structure of Religious Experience*, 11. The notion of being "tied at both ends" suggests a close congruence with American pragmatism, but as we have noted earlier, Macmurray was apparently both ignorant of the work of James, Peirce, and Dewey and highly critical of what he took to be a much narrower philosophy of pragmatism in which one determined truth simply by the success of whatever one desired.

31. Macmurray, *The Structure of Religious Experience*, 33.

32. Macmurray, *The Structure of Religious Experience*, 46.

33. Macmurray, *The Structure of Religious Experience*, 50.

34. Macmurray, *The Structure of Religious Experience*, 50.

35. Macmurray, *The Structure of Religious Experience*, 50.

36. Macmurray, *The Structure of Religious Experience*, 50–51.

37. Macmurray, *The Structure of Religious Experience*, 51.

38. Macmurray, *The Structure of Religious Experience*, 51.

39. Macmurray, *The Structure of Religious Experience*, 51.

40. Macmurray, *The Structure of Religious Experience*, 51.

41. See J. Glenn Gray, ed., *G. W. F. Hegel: On Art, Religion, Philosophy* (New York: Harper Torchbook, 1970), note 3: *aufgehoben*, 141.

42. Macmurray, *The Structure of Religious Experience*, 74.

43. Macmurray, *The Structure of Religious Experience*, 74.

44. Macmurray, *Religion in the Modern World*, 1.

45. Macmurray, *Religion in the Modern World*, 2.

46. Macmurray, *Religion in the Modern World*, 8.

47. Macmurray, *Religion in the Modern World*, 13–14.

48. Macmurray, *Religion in the Modern World*, 14.

49. Macmurray, *Religion in the Modern World*, 18.

50. John Macmurray, *Freedom in the Modern World* (London: Faber and Faber, 1932): "real feeling grasps the value of what is not ourselves, and enjoys it or disapproves it. The moment that feeling ceases to be directed outwards, the moment it ceases to be an appreciation of the thing or the person with which it is connected in fact, it becomes unreal" (147).

51. Macmurray, *Religion in the Modern World*, 18.

52. Macmurray, *Religion in the Modern World*, 18.

53. John Macmurray, "The Religious Task of the Christian Left," *Christian Left*, March 20, 1937, 4.

54. John Macmurray et al., "The New Magazine, October, 1937," "Christian Left Documents," "The Christian Left: Draft Basis," "Cross, Hammer and Sickle," "The Summer Conference," in *Christian Left*, July 15, 1937, 4.

55. John Macmurray, "The Provisional Basis of the Christian Left," *Christian Left*, February 1938, 4.

56. Macmurray, "The Provisional Basis of the Christian Left," 6.

57. Macmurray, "The Provisional Basis of the Christian Left," 6.

58. Macmurray, "The Religious Task of the Christian Left," 4.

59. Macmurray, "The Religious Task of the Christian Left," 5.

60. Macmurray, "The Provisional Basis of the Christian Left," 4.

61. John Macmurray, "Has Religion a Message for To-Day?" *Reynolds's Illustrated News*, November 24, 1935.

62. Macmurray, "The Religious Task of the Christian Left," 4.

63. Macmurray, "The Provisional Basis of the Christian Left," 5.

64. Macmurray, "The Provisional Basis of the Christian Left," 5.

65. John Macmurray, "Russia and Finland," *Christian Left*, March 1940, 6.

66. John Macmurray, "Religion in Russia," Anglo-Soviet Public Relations Association, Leaflet 1, 1942, 1.

67. Macmurray, "Religion in Russia," 2.

68. John Macmurray, "Valuations in Fascist and Community States," in T. H. Marshall, ed., *Class Conflict and Social Stratification* (London: LePlay House Press, 1938), 18–191.

69. John Macmurray, *The Boundaries of Science* (London: Faber and Faber, 1939). Given his focus on the nature of persons in relation, it is not surprising to discover that the science Macmurray found most attractive was psychology. He even regarded economics as one of the psychological sciences because it studies human behavior in a particular field (63–65). His underlying premise was that science is perfectly adequate to study the nonpersonal, organic, or material dimensions of personal life but that, at least in terms of a closed system of cause and effect, it cannot account for the intentionality that lies behind all human activity, including the intentionality that guides scientific investigation itself. Macmurray's understanding of psychology was remarkably similar to that developed by "object-relations" theorists, one of whom, Harry Guntrip, was directly indebted to Macmurray, and another of whom, W. R. D. Fairbairn, was a contemporary of his in Scotland.

70. Macmurray, "Valuations in Fascist and Community States," 182–83.

71. Macmurray, "Valuations in Fascist and Community States," 184.

72. Macmurray, "Valuations in Fascist and Community States," 185.

73. Macmurray, "Valuations in Fascist and Community States," 187.

74. See John Costello, *John Macmurray: A Biography* (Edinburgh: Floris Books, 2002), 275–78.

75. John Macmurray, "Socialism and Democracy," *Christian Left*, March 1940, 1.

76. Macmurray, "Socialism and Democracy," 1–2.

77. Macmurray, "Socialism and Democracy," 2.

78. Macmurray, "Socialism and Democracy," 3.

79. John Macmurray, *Constructive Democracy* (London: Faber and Faber, 1943).

80. Macmurray, *Constructive Democracy*, 7. He dismissed the relevance of the Russian experiment, noting that it had gone from a barely industrialized autocracy to a fully industrialized democracy (at least in theory), and had failed to make the movement with its democratic principles intact.

81. Macmurray, *Constructive Democracy*, 11.

82. Macmurray, *Constructive Democracy*, 13.

83. Macmurray, *Constructive Democracy*, 14–15. Macmurray continually slips back and forth in his use of the word "community," sometimes confusing it with society, from which he has earlier been at pains to distinguish it. He won't really clear up this confusion in *terminology* until the Gifford Lectures, but there was no confusion in the meaning he gave to the *concepts* of society and community even prior to this time.

84. Macmurray, *Constructive Democracy*, 16.

85. Macmurray, *Constructive Democracy*, 16.

86. Macmurray, *Constructive Democracy*, 17–18.

87. Macmurray, *Constructive Democracy*, 21. As we shall see, in this respect Macmurray, despite his repeated emphasis on "community," is actually much closer to

the liberal tradition of Rawls than he is to the "communitarian" tradition of other contemporary political philosophers such as MacIntyre and Sandel.

88. Macmurray, *Constructive Democracy*, 30.

89. Macmurray, *Constructive Democracy*, 33.

90. Macmurray, *Constructive Democracy*, 37.

91. Macmurray, *Constructive Democracy*, 37.

92. Macmurray, *Constructive Democracy*, 38.

93. Macmurray, *Constructive Democracy*, 40.

94. Macmurray, *Constructive Democracy*, 41.

95. John Macmurray, "Freedom in the Personal Nexus," in *Freedom: Its Meaning*, ed. Ruth Nanda Anshen (New York: Harcourt Brace, 1940), 176–93.

96. John Macmurray, *Conditions of Freedom* (London: Faber and Faber, 1950). The lectures on which the book was based took place in 1949 as the "Second Lectures of the Chancellor Dunning Trust, Queen's University, Kingston, Ontario."

97. Macmurray, "Freedom in the Personal Nexus," 185.

98. Macmurray, "Freedom in the Personal Nexus," 191.

99. Macmurray, "Freedom in the Personal Nexus," 192.

100. Macmurray, "Freedom in the Personal Nexus," 193.

101. Richard Acland, *Questions and Answers from Common Wealth Meetings* (London, 1943), 21.

102. Richard Acland, *Nothing Left to Believe?* (London: Longmans Green, 1949), 75, 104.

103. For more on Common Wealth, see G. D. H. Cole, *A History of the Labour Party from 1914* (London: Routledge and Kegan Paul, 1948), 400–11; and Angus Calder, *The People's War* (New York: Pantheon and Random House, 1969), 546–50. There is an especially intriguing letter by George Orwell in August 1942 commenting on C.W. He says it should not be taken seriously. He refers to Acland's pamphlets as "baby language" and the movement as "Socialism minus the class war and with the emphasis on the moral instead of the economic motive." He notes that one of the appeals of C.W. is that it avoids Marxism, proletarian dictatorship, and any disparagement of patriotism. (London Letter to *Partisan Review*, August 29 1942, in *The Collected Essays, Journalism and Letters of George Orwell*, vol. 2, *My Country Right or Left 1940–1943*, ed. Sonia Orwell and Ian Angus (New York: Harcourt, Brace and World, 1968), 230–32.

104. Macmurray, *Conditions of Freedom*, 10.

105. Macmurray, *Conditions of Freedom*, 16.

106. Macmurray, *Conditions of Freedom*, 19. This was the theme of *The Clue to History*, in which he argues that unless we align our intentions with those of God, we will not be able to achieve our purposes.

107. Macmurray, *Conditions of Freedom*, 32.

108. Macmurray, *Conditions of Freedom*, 39.

109. Macmurray, *Conditions of Freedom*, 41. He notes that this faith is undiminished by the fact that he has never voted for someone who won an election in the United Kingdom.

110. Macmurray, *Conditions of Freedom*, 42.

111. A fuller treatment of Macmurray's ideas on transcending the nation-state will be taken up in the final chapter of this book.

6

THE GIFFORD LECTURES:
THE SELF AS AGENT

The full flowering of Macmurray's political philosophy is found in what is arguably his most influential work, the Gifford Lectures of 1953–1954, given at the University of Glasgow and published in two volumes, *The Self as Agent*[1] and *Persons in Relation*.[2] Not surprisingly, given the careful way he has crafted the relation between politics and his overarching notion of community, Macmurray's detailed treatment of politics occurs toward the conclusion of the development of what he calls the "form of the personal." The metaphysical and practical (they are never divorced in Macmurray) thesis of this philosophical form is, simply stated, that "all meaningful knowledge is for the sake of action, and all meaningful action is for the sake of friendship."[3] A philosophical form, on the basis of which this thesis will be elaborated, is a way of representing or exhibiting the unity of human experience as a whole.[4]

The bold, even startling character of the enterprise he set himself in the Giffords is acknowledged by Macmurray himself. In attempting to establish a new philosophical form, he is deliberately setting himself against the mainstream traditions of Western philosophy, especially those represented by Descartes and Kant. And he knows that he will not always be successful in eradicating from the new form elements of the older forms of thought he wants to reject. "The influence of the old assumptions is pervasive and unformulated. It is not possible, even if were desirable, to empty one's mind completely and start afresh in a condition of intellectual innocence. It is only to be expected, therefore, that I have carried over much from the old order that should have been left behind, and that my tentative theorizing will be found liable, at many points, to the objection that it still presupposes what it purports to reject."[5]

He asserts that what is driving his search for a new philosophical form is the "crisis of the personal." What he means by this is that the political state has become too overweening and the role of religion too reduced in the modern age and nation-state.[6] Although he will emphasize the importance of community as a solution to the "apotheosis" of the state, it is clear that he also wants to stress the centrality of the individual in that communal relationship. The problem with the modern political state, he argues, is that it removes too much of individual responsibility and subordinates the individual to his or her functionality within an organic whole that cannot value the unique, nonfunctional dimension of the self. In this respect he unabashedly commits himself to the political philosophy of liberalism, which was, he says, "an effort, however ambiguous, to subordinate the functional organization of society to the personal life of its members."[7] At the same time he recalls the communist charge that while liberalism may have the right values, in practice it often winds up accepting the power of the state over the individual in the defense of exploiting the poor by the rich (i.e., through what he has called "negative democracy"). Communism has also fallen victim to the practice of subordinating the personal to the functional. What is needed is a new philosophical form that can rescue the personal from a betrayal that comes not primarily through the theories of communism or liberalism, but through their practice.

At the heart of the philosophical form that Macmurray wants to reject are two assumptions, both of which he will challenge. First is the assumption that the self is to be defined primarily in and through its reflective activities, that is, as a thinker. The second assumption is that the self is primarily and essentially an individual whose identity is not drawn from complex interrelations with other beings. He wants to replace these assumptions with two that, on the surface, seem deceptively simple: first, that the self is primarily an agent (only one of whose actions is reflective), and second, that the self is a *relational* being whose very essence is found primarily in deep intimate relations with other persons but with whom one must also relate in indirect, formal, and less intimate ways. This second form of relationality will be at the heart of the political enterprise.

A word of caution is helpful at this point. Macmurray relies very heavily on the words "person," "personal," and "community." These terms carry very heavy psychological and rhetorical freight these days. Perhaps because we *are* persons, we find the words referring to persons both attractive and vague at the same time. They cover a host of meanings, which are very difficult to unpack and clarify. The caution is to remember that Macmurray is treating the concept of the person as a philosophical, even metaphysical notion, and the heart of a philosophical form. "Person" will have very specific meanings within the context of his overarching philosophy. We need to let the elements of this philosophy take their place in the metaphysical whole before rushing to a premature (and false) judgment that the term "personal" is too slippery, loose, vague, or rhetorical to undergird a complex, subtle, and logical philosophical understanding of reality. Macmurray insists that he is making a serious contribution to philosophical theory, and he uses the formal language of much contemporary philosophy to do so.

The Gifford Lectures were an ideal occasion to develop the philosophy of the personal because at its heart is the activity of religious reflection and action. The Giffords were intended to be a reflection on "natural" theology (i.e., one that does not rely primarily on "revealed" data within a religious tradition). Macmurray was a fully realized natural theologian or philosopher. The role of religion and the role of politics were much more tightly integrated (though clearly distinguishable) in his thought than they would have been in the mind of a doctrinal or revealed theologian. The role that religion plays in his developed philosophy is a practical one (though it has a reflective component), as are the roles that politics, economics, morality, and art play.[8] But religion, as a phenomenon, remains subject to philosophical investigation even though it is not, itself, primarily reflective. And the category of the personal is one that yields itself to such investigation even while it is *the* crucial category for understanding the importance of religion (and derivatively of politics as well).

It is also important to remember how crucial the dialectic between theory and practice has been for Macmurray ever since his early work on Marx. This dialectic is at the heart of the philosophy of the personal. It means that human beings take thought in order to make their practice better able to achieve their intentions in the world of objective entities. At the risk of sounding outlandish, Macmurray even asserts that if a purely theoretical activity intends no reference to the practical life, it is imaginary and an exercise of "phantasy." The "truth or falsity of the theoretical is to be found solely in its reference to the practical."[9]

Macmurray then rehearses the central themes he first outlined in the late 1920s regarding the inadequacies of the mathematical (physical or material) and organic models (what he had called "unity-patterns" in *Interpreting the Universe*) for understanding the person. Both fail to do justice to the self because, while appropriate in limited respects, they do not capture what is uniquely personal in human beings, namely their intentionality[10] and their capacity for forming mutual loving relationships (friendship) in community. Both forms leave out the fact that persons are embedded in relationships.

They try to think of the self as isolated from those relationships and, therefore, begin on a completely inadequate note. What Macmurray wants to do is think from the standpoint of the self as a relational being.[11]

This first leads him into a detailed analysis of Kantian philosophy, which he sees as beginning with theoretical reason and winding up affirming the primacy of practical reason (even if this was not Kant's original intention). Kant had hoped to find a standpoint within thought by which the self could guarantee the truth of its conceptual understanding of the world. Through the transcendental unity of apperception or forms of intuition, the self is assured that the forms of thought do apply to what it perceives (even though it cannot know the object that lies behind the perception as it is in itself). But a high price is paid for the certainty of understanding what appears to us through the forms of apperception. That price is the subordination of what we perceive to the determinative laws of cause and effect. These laws have no place for uniquely human freedom. But Kant knows that when we are held morally accountable for our actions, we must presuppose freedom of will and action. This creates a paradox or dualism that can only be overcome, not in thought, but in action itself.

According to Macmurray, the key to transcending the Kantian dualism between theory and action is by dismantling Kant's notion of the unknowability of the "thing-in-itself." Since the transcendental forms of intuition provide the necessary framework through which our perceptions of the empirical world must pass in order to attain the status of knowledge, there must be, according to Kant, a gap between the "true" reality of the objects that are being perceived and the knowledge we have of them based on those perceptions. We never get to "see" the object being perceived as it is in itself, since it is always filtered by the forms of intuition.

Macmurray faults Kant for failing to provide a satisfactory explanation of human freedom (which Kant admits that we "know" whenever we act morally) in a world that must be known conceptually as devoid of such freedom insofar as it conflicts with causal law. It will not do to resolve this antinomy by resorting to a fundamental dualism between what we know and what we do. The two "worlds" of Kant, the noumenal and the phenomenal, cannot in the end be radically dualistic worlds for the unified self, because the self has to live in both. The problem facing the philosopher is how to think of both worlds as a single world for a single self.

If, of course, I have begun my philosophical project by thinking of myself essentially and primarily as a thinker, as one who must first "think" the unity of the noumenal and phenomenal worlds, then I can't help but wind up where Kant did: in a dualism between what I think and know conceptually and what I do and know in action. Kant winds up arguing that we can only know ourselves as able to act freely in the world if we "think" of reason, in the end, as primarily practical. In and through our moral actions we somehow "know" that we are free (since morality presupposes freedom). And we know that we are moral because we feel the compulsion of the moral law within us. In Kant's view, we can only accept from our practice the conclusion that we are free: we cannot know it from theory. The gap between theory and practice is bridged by faith, not reason.

This pushes us back to the fundamental problem: the initial dualism in Kant (and earlier in Descartes) between theory and practice. Both Kant and Descartes have started with the assumption that the self is primarily a thinker who must account for itself through thought. Macmurray believes that any philosophy that takes the cogito as its starting point "institutes a formal dualism of theory and practice: and that this dualism makes it formally impossible to give any account, and indeed to conceive the possibility of persons in relation, whether the relation be theoretical—as knowledge, or practical—as co-operation."[12] Thinking cannot establish relationality: it can, at best, reflect it. But relationality is essentially action, not ideation. It comes about through what we *do*, not through what we think (though thinking can be instrumental for action). And here is the heart of the problem. If the essential characteristic of the self is thinking, and if thinking determines what is real, then action becomes a mystery that, as Kant understood, we have to believe in but which we cannot comprehend. Thinking about an action does not constitute that action. Thinking about a relationship does not constitute the relationship. Macmurray says that while philosophy must be theoretical, it does not follow that it must theorize from the standpoint of theory. He believes it can theorize from the standpoint of action.

It follows, he argues, that we need to reverse the traditional relationship between thought and action and begin with the assumption that the primary characteristic of the self is agency. All philosophies that start with the cogito "presuppose the primacy of the theoretical. They conceive reason at once as the differentia of the personal, as that which constitutes the human organism a 'self.'"[13] But the contradiction involved in starting with the cogito is that it claims both that the chief characteristic of the self is *thought* and that thinking is the chief *action* of the self. But if the self is primarily an agent, then it is, by virtue of that fact, already embedded in an external world of relationships. The existence of the self precedes any thinking that the self does (in part because, unless there was already a world in which the self existed, there would be nothing about which to think in the first place). Thought, in and of itself, does not have effects upon that world. Thinking then, in Macmurray's terms, is a negative activity in relation to the positive activities of the self, which are "material, causal and effective in the modification of the not-self." To exist is to be part of the external world "in systematic causal relation with other parts of the world."[14] To exist as agent is to exist through the "full concrete activity of the self in which all our capacities are employed."[15]

Thinking is one activity of the self, but one in which the self is temporarily withdrawn from its inclusive engagement with the world of which it is a part. Action is the more inclusive characteristic of the self: as an ideal it is "the concept of an unlimited rational being, in which all the capacities of the Self are in full and unrestricted employment."[16] Of course this is an ideal and rarely, if ever, realized by any existing self. As inclusive, however, action in a rational being will include thinking as a component part. Thinking serves the intentions of the self by informing and guiding them in terms of what it believes is true or false. Action, on the other hand, is determined by what is right or wrong. This means that the "moral" distinction is the primary standard of validity, while the epistemological distinction (true or false) is secondary and derivative.

This way of putting things eliminates the need for the Kantian distinction between the thing-in-itself and the thing as it appears to us. Both thinking and acting take place in and refer to the same world. And, for Macmurray, action is not taking place when there is no thought that informs it. Mere movement or unconscious behavior is not action.[17] Action presumes some degree of theory or knowledge.

In his development of the concept of the self as agent, Macmurray reverts to the language of negative and positive he had used earlier under Hegelian influence. He also uses the word "subject" for the self only with respect to its thinking activity (perhaps trying to distance himself from existentialism's retreat from reason). He says, for example, that the self "exists" only as agent and that the "negative" aspect of the self is when it is "subject" (i.e., when it is thinking). The points is he trying to make are valid, but calling thinking "negative" is misleading and unhelpful.

Given that our existence as selves is embedded in the practical world of external objective others, it follows that the philosophy of the personal must take up the question of our perception of those others. Perhaps not surprisingly, but certainly against the stream of traditional epistemology, Macmurray suggests that the primary mode of perception is touch, not sight. Sight does not give me a basis for distinguishing between a perception of the other as "real" or as "illusory." Sight, being primarily receptive, makes no difference in the object being seen. However, if the self is primarily agent, then touch does make such a difference. "Tactual perception is *necessarily* perception in action. To touch anything is to exert pressure on it . . . to modify it."[18] In that modification, I "know" I am in contact with something other than myself.

At this point Macmurray, still in the mode of the philosophical development of a metaphysical way of understanding the world, introduces an idea that will be crucial to the development of his political philosophy: resistance. According to Macmurray, "The core of tactual perception is the experience of resistance"[19] by an other. I know when I've met the objective reality of something other than myself when it frustrates my will when I am in the process of enacting it. "Tactual perception, as the experience of resistance, is the direct and immediate apprehension of the Other-than-myself. The Other is that which resists my will."[20] Conversely, I also know myself as that which resists the other.

This is a crucial concept for a couple of reasons. First, it avoids the sentimental notion that personal relationships ought to encourage persons to blend or meld themselves into one. Resistance to the other is always going to be part of any healthy relationship. Second, it provides the foundation for an understanding of political life as the negotiation of competing, resisting forces. Society (the arena in which political philosophy is most obviously instantiated) is then both well justified (since resistance is not only inevitable but also necessary for the full realization of the self) and at the same time distinguishable from community (in which resistance, while never absent, is subordinated to the intentionality of the inclusive embrace of love and mutuality). Resistance of and by the other is the evidence of my existence and character as a relational being. Resistance is also necessary for there to be action at all, because to act is to act *upon* something.[21]

Resistance can be either positive or negative from my standpoint. It is negative when it stubbornly resists an intention of mine that would, if realized, enhance my possibilities of flourishing. It is positive when it forces me to take account of the uniqueness of the other that is resisting me. It forces me to acknowledge that I am not alone and must, to be fulfilled, enter into the most positive relationship with the other of which we are both capable.

Once I have encountered the other through tactual perception and the experience of its resistance, I need to conceptually characterize it correctly if I am to act effectively in relation to it. Macmurray believes that the original (though revisable) characterization of the other is that it is an agent like myself. "I must attribute to the Other, if I am to understand it, the form of activity that I attribute to myself."[22] Through a kind of trial and error, in continuing interaction with the other, I discover *in practice* which character-izations are appropriate. If I characterize the Other as another personal agent and it turns out that it is a tree, my mental concept will prove ineffi-cacious in guiding my practical dealings with it.[23] As a personal agent I in-clude in my being materiality, organism, and the distinguishing trait of the person: intentionality and the capacity to act. Through ongoing experience of the other, I may well discover that it has neither organic nor intentional faculties (say it is a rock). Its resistance is not intentional. If, however, I de-termine that the other is an agent like myself, then I characterize the form of its resistance as a personal will in opposition to mine. This is the founda-tion of morality: "the distinction between right and wrong depends upon a clash of wills."[24]

One crucial implication Macmurray draws from this analysis of the perception of the other is that, in and through our experience, we know the difference between explanations of actions and of events. Actions only make sense when explained by the intention of the agent. Events, which do not have agents as their source, can be caused entirely by nonintentional forces. The conception of a cause is the conception of an action with the element of intentionality excluded from it.   .

Knowledge of causality (absent intentionality) is the proper domain of science. Its field is the world of the "continuant," as Macmurray puts it. Continuance is the character of unchangingness, subject to what we con-strue as the laws of Nature. Their applicability as laws is limited by the pro-viso: "provided nothing interferes." But the interference of the agent "into" the laws of nature is a signal part of human experience. (Interference does not mean violation or contravention of the laws of nature). "All our physi-cal predictions depend on an abstraction from the presence of agents, with their capacity to determine the future" by their intentional actions.[25]

Intentional actions require a degree of theoretical knowledge. This is attained, according to Macmurray, by the negative action of reflection.[26] I need to know something *about* the other if I intend to modify either its be-havior or my own. I need to know conceptually "the variations of resistance to my movement in different directions" with respect to the other.[27] So I intend, as a means to an end, to withdraw from a full active engagement with the other into a moment of reflection. I must now *attend* to the other (or some aspect of it) so as to adjust or develop a better conceptual repre-sentation of it if my ongoing actions in relation to it are to be more likely to achieve my intentions. Of course, "the constructs produced by selective attention, and the conclusions of reflective processes of thought equally re-quire verification by reference to practical experience."[28]

Macmurray notes in this context that the origin or beginning of any withdrawal into reflective thought is feeling. I feel a sense of dissatisfaction in my relationship with the other: something is felt as being amiss; harmony, unity, is absent. My intentions are being frustrated. If my theory has been successfully verified, then I feel satisfaction at the end of the process. These feelings, that both begin and terminate the process of action-withdrawal-return, are valuations of the relationship and of the object with which I am in relation. Feeling always refers to an object (not just my inner state). And it can be objectively right or wrong, as Macmurray had argued earlier in *Reason and Emotion*. There is such a thing as emotional knowledge. Its goal is to know the world as an end-in-itself, to enjoy the world for its own sake.[29]

Macmurray concludes *The Self as Agent* with reflections on the idea of God, which need not detain us here because they are not central to the development of his political philosophy. Put succinctly, he believes a metaphysic of action (which is central to his philosophy of the personal) requires us to "think" the world as one action. If we wish to think the unity of the world (a metaphysical imperative), he argues, then we need to think it as a unity of action by all the agents comprised within it. A unity of action is, necessarily, a unity of intention. Therefore we should act "as though our own actions were our contributions to the one inclusive action which is the history of the world."[30] The significance of this "theological" reference is simply that our actions, personal, economic, political, or otherwise, must be guided by the belief that we are contributing to the unity of the world and are in conformity with the overarching intention built into it (by God, according to Macmurray). This leads directly into the problem he takes up in *Persons in Relation*, namely the constitution of personal relationships at both the societal and the communal levels.

NOTES

1. John Macmurray, *The Self as Agent* (London: Faber and Faber, 1957); reprinted, with an introduction by Stanley M. Harrison (London: Humanities Press International, 1991).

2. John Macmurray, *Persons in Relation* (New York: Harper and Brothers, 1961); reprinted, with an introduction by Frank G. Kirkpatrick (London: Humanities Press International, 1991).

3. Macmurray, *The Self as Agent*, 15.

4. Macmurray, *The Self as Agent*, 13.

5. Macmurray, *The Self as Agent*, 14. I will suggest some places in his work that are, in fact, examples of his retention of the philosophical forms he is attempting to reject.

6. Macmurray, *The Self as Agent*, 29.

7. Macmurray, *The Self as Agent*, 30.

8. It might not be unfair to avoid using the word "theology" to describe Macmurray's work. Especially when theology was assumed to rely on revealed truths, it is inappropriate to think of Macmurray as a theologian. His data were always the data of human history and the natural world. When most people in the United Kingdom would think of Karl Barth's revealed, dogmatic theology as the embodiment of what religious thinkers did, it is important to remember that Macmurray was first and foremost a philosopher. He challenges philosophy to take the realities of God and religion seriously, and in this respect he was outside the mainstream of British philosophy during his time as well. Macmurray saw the differences between his thought and that of Barth quite clearly. He said at one point that trying to combine Barth and himself is like trying to combine capitalism and democracy. Barth's emphasis on the transcendence of God releases both God and human beings from their responsibilities for history. See John Costello, *John Macmurray: A Biography* (Edinburgh: Floris Books, 2002), 270. Macmurray's comments are from a letter to his friend Richard Roberts in 1936. Costello notes that Macmurray later revised his view of Barth when he spoke favorably of the latter's challenge to Nazism (414, note 19).

9. Macmurray, *The Self as Agent*, 2–22. This bald assertion is immediately qualified when Macmurray admits that not only is the reference of theory to practice not always obvious or direct but also that "the disinterested pursuit of truth may be . . . a condition of the practical efficacy of reflection" (*The Self as Agent*, 22–23). Nevertheless, his key point stands that reflection must be tied at some point and in some ways to practical life. "It is always legitimate to ask, of any theory which claims to be true, what practical difference it would make if we believed it" (*The Self as Agent*, 23).

10. It should be clear that by the word "intentionality" Macmurray means the intention that stands behind or guides the action of an agent. He does not mean it in the sense used by contemporary phenomenological philosophy as referring primarily to concepts or ideas that are "about" something other than themselves.

11. To think from a standpoint means that Macmurray intentionally steps back in reflection to think about what it means to be a self that can step back in reflection. And it means, for him, that the self is then seen as primarily an agent, one of whose actions is this stepping back. Using thought to discover the centrality of agency is not a contradiction in terms, since the purpose of thought is to understand reality as it is, and this he believes he has done through the form of the personal.

12. Macmurray, *The Self as Agent*, 73.

13. Macmurray, *The Self as Agent*, 79.

14. Macmurray, *The Self as Agent*, 80–81.

15. Macmurray, *The Self as Agent*, 86.

16. Macmurray, *The Self as Agent*, 87.

17. This restriction of the concept of action to that which carries a conscious intention or idea into practice does not conform to a lot of contemporary thinking in the social sciences. But it is Macmurray's understanding of action, and this must be kept in mind in order to appreciate what he does with the concept.

18. Macmurray, *The Self as Agent*, 107.

19. Macmurray, *The Self as Agent*, 108.

20. Macmurray, *The Self as Agent*, 109.

21. Macmurray, *The Self as Agent*, 110.

22. Macmurray, *The Self as Agent*, 116.

23. Unless, of course, it turns out to be one of Tolkein's "ents," which are trees with consciousness and some degree of agency.

24. Macmurray, *The Self as Agent*, 145.

25. Macmurray, *The Self as Agent*, 159.

26. "Negative" in this context simply means that theory is a prerequisite for action, and action is more basic, more fulfilling, more expressive of the self than is the "sub-act" of thinking, which is subordinate to the successful carrying out of intentional acts in the world that intend a modification of the external and objective other.

27. Macmurray, *The Self as Agent*, 166.

28. Macmurray, *The Self as Agent*, 174.

29. Much in what Macmurray says about emotion tracks closely with the thought of Alfred North Whitehead and the process philosophers and theologians who have been instructed by him. We will say more about the importance of recognizing emotional knowledge later.

30. Macmurray, *The Self as Agent*, 221. I have discussed at various other places Macmurray's notion of God as the agent whose overarching intention constitutes the unity of the world and do not intend to bring in those ideas at this point.

7

THE GIFFORD LECTURES:
PERSONS IN RELATION

In the second volume of the Gifford Lectures, *Persons in Relation*, Macmurray developed his principal themes of community and personal relationship. His underlying premise was that "the Self is constituted by its relation to the Other; that it has its being in its relationship; and that this relationship is necessarily personal."[1] Central to this premise was his claim that all such relationships have negative and positive aspects. The negative aspect is the impersonal dimension of relationality, and it is always present in any relationship. The impersonal dimension is present when we have to treat others instrumentally or without entering into a fully personal relation with them. I do not have a fully personal relationship with the person who delivers my newspaper, and thus the relation is primarily impersonal or functional. There are, however, no absolutely or exclusively personal or impersonal relations with other persons. The context and the intentions behind the relationship determine its degree of impersonality. If in some situations I regard others impersonally, I can treat them as objects to be studied as parts of the causal chain that links all objects under scientific laws (as "continuants"). And it is certainly true that all of us are in some way subject to objective analysis in which our full personhood is not taken into account. Persons cannot be fulfilled only through impersonal relations, but the impersonal must be present in the other if we are to have an objective knowledge of him or her.

We can also relate to others either directly or indirectly. All indirect relations are necessarily impersonal (I may never see, except at a distance, the paper deliverer). Direct relations, where we meet face to face and may become personally acquainted with each other, can be either primarily personal or impersonal, depending on the intentions of the parties. The fullness of human relationship comes only in relations that are primarily personal and direct (though again, Macmurray insisted, even these relations will have a negative aspect of the impersonal and the objective contained within them). This claim is important because it means that, beyond the smallest kinds of mutual communities in which direct personal relations are the norm, all social or political relationships are going to be impersonal and usually indirect. The key to characterizing relationships is the intention behind them, since the possibility of impersonal, indirect, direct, or personal relationships is not determined by the mere fact of being in contact with another person.

The intentionality of relationships also contains a crucial emotional component. In a chapter that reveals Macmurray's sensitivity to the role of emotions in the development of personal relationships, he discussed the "inherently personal" (even primordial) relationship between mother and child in which "embracing love" by the mother is the chief characteristic.[2] The infant can, at first, only live through the intentional activity of its mother. (The infant is driven by not yet fully developed intentional motives, but the mother relates to her child in a fully intentional way, which still has a motivational component, since she is always free to abandon the child and the relationship. Eventually the child's motivations can become intentional once it reaches a certain degree of maturity.) If the child is to grow into consciousness and intentionality it must be nurtured to do so by the mother. Thus Macmurray concluded, the "unit of personal existence is not the individual, but two persons in personal relation. . . . The personal is constituted by personal relatedness. The unit of the personal is not the 'I' but the 'You and I.'"[3] Crucially, he argued, the relation between mother and child is enjoyed for its own sake. It is not a means to an end but an end in itself. This is the fullness of relationship: to enjoy the other for the other's own sake and for the intrinsic joy of the relationship itself.

Central to the development of the full personhood of the infant is its ability to "*discriminate* the Other" *as* other. At first the infant regards everything as an extension of itself, but when parts of the other don't respond appropriately to the impulses of the child, the child learns to discriminate the other from itself into the not-self. The first other the infant discriminates is the mother. Initially it is motivated toward the mother by the two basic motives of love and fear. Through these motives, it seeks from the other the satisfaction of needs by an appropriate response from the other to whom they are directed. This is what Macmurray called the "*mutuality* of the personal."[4]

Just as there are positive and negative dimensions in our relations with others, so there are positive and negative dimensions in our motivations toward them. The positive motivation (meaning the one that comes closest to realizing the fullness of the person) is that of love. It is a love *of and for* the other for his or her own sake. The negative motivation is fear, fear *of* the other and *for* oneself. The primary fear is that the other will not respond to my need in a way that truly satisfies it and, as a result, my intentions will be frustrated. Out of this fear for myself I develop a fear of the other as a threat to me. And yet this fear presupposes love (since love alone can satisfy the self) and is thus "subordinate" to love.[5] But no actions can be motivated solely or exhaustively by fear, which, being essentially defensive and egocentric, would cut off the very relationship through which the self can be fulfilled. In order to do something about my fear, I need to have some positive motivation to reach out to the other.

Macmurray introduces at this point the elusive but critical concept of "heterocentricity." It means, in contrast to egocentricity (in which the object of one's concern is oneself), that the other is the center of one's concern. To act toward the other for the sake of the other is heterocentric and is a positively motivated action. When one is heterocentrically oriented toward the other, love dominates fear (though it does not extinguish it). The child, unless it has been severely traumatized by an uncaring, egocentrically motivated mother, will subordinate the negative motivation of fear within a "persistently positive motivation" of love toward the mother.[6]

Hatred of the other derives from love and fear. When my actions (motivated by love) are rebuffed or frustrated, when mutuality is refused, then my personal existence is frustrated absolutely. To some degree all relationships will have hatred and fear as components because, as Macmurray puts it, it is "impossible that you should always be able to respond to me in the way that my action expects."[7] On the other hand, if I am the one to reject a personal, direct overture from a loving other, then I will frustrate my own being. Thus hatred and fear are negative motivations that cannot be universalized, since they would destroy the very essence of what it means to be a person.

As the child's relationship with the mother grows, the child acquires greater practical sophistication in discriminating the nature of its particular mother and, later, of the multiple others with whom it is in contact. When the other does not respond personally, then the child has reason to conclude that *this* other is not a person (or is a person choosing not to respond personally). Consequently the child's actions in relation to this other (e.g., a bottle) will be different from those in relation to its loving mother. Essentially the discrimination of the nature of the other is by a "*reduction of the concept of the [personal] Other which excludes part of its definition . . . by a partial* negation: only by down-grading the 'You' in the 'You and I' to the status of 'It.'"[8] The nonpersonal other then becomes the correlate of the self as and to the extent that it is also nonpersonal, that is, as an object or body only.[9] In its relation to the bottle, the child need intend nothing personally, but only instrumentally and impersonally.

The nonpersonal other is that in the other which does not respond personally to my personal call to it. "The relation I have with it lacks the mutuality of a personal relation." It corresponds to the nonintentional, nonagent part of myself. When it resists me, it does so not as an agent, but passively, as a material or organic object. It becomes, in effect, a means for me to carry out my intentions in relation to other agents but is not itself an agent.[10]

All personal relationships seem destined to fail at some point, for longer or shorter periods of time. If I am rebuffed by the personal other or feel isolated from it, I become egocentric, fearful, defensive, and in extreme cases fall into despair. Only if the personal other can break through my defensive shell can I be restored to a loving relationship, assuming I accept the overture. But the restoration of relationality requires an initial breaking away from the other, allowing the negative dimension of relationship (fear) to gain the upper hand. Nevertheless, I cannot be a fully relational being unless I can experience my own identity as an individual self, not simply a dependent self made in the image of the other. If I am to be a full, intentional, and contributing member to the relationship, I must retreat from it temporarily, hoping to restore it on a different or better basis. In the process, Macmurray insisted, I will discover myself as an individual and through that discovery become a more mature and full person.

RESISTANCE TO THE OTHER

The process of becoming a mature person involves the crucial notion of *resistance* to the other. Macmurray was quite clear that personal relations do not involve the submerging of the individuality of the persons in relation: they require its enhancement. Only by experiencing and offering resistance to the other can the child discover himself "as an individual by contrasting himself, and indeed willfully opposing himself to the family *to which he belongs*; and this *discovery* of his individuality is at the same time the *realization* of his individuality."[11] This is the rhythm of withdrawal and return that is essential for any healthy growth of individuality (and is as true for societies as it is for individuals, an issue we will take up shortly.)

Withdrawal from the other becomes the basis of the moral struggle: there is an opposition to be overcome, a conflict of wills to be resolved. This opposition helps the child recognize himself or herself as an agent through the experience of an opposing agent who seeks to subordinate the child to its will. The will of the other must be met by the child's counter-will. This clash of wills gives rise to a series of dichotomies between real and unreal, right and wrong, good and evil, true and false. And the problematic they present to the self is that of reconciliation, of overcoming the fear of the other without subordinating oneself in a servile manner to the other by a refusal to accept one's own individuality and distinctness.

Normally, the first others (beyond the mother) that the child discriminates are the members of a family. They constitute the first community the child experiences and of which he comes to believe he is a loved member. Macmurray gave an extraordinary value to the family, which he said is both the "model for all other communities" and for any more inclusive group of persons conceived as a personal whole.[12] He believed that the family is the "original human community and the basis as well as the origin of all subsequent communities. It is therefore the norm of all community, so that any community is a brotherhood."[13]

If the child successfully negotiates his or her encounter with the discriminated others in the family, the next move is to conceive the way by which conflicting intentions can be reconciled. In a world of multiple personal others, this conception is that of a unity of action or intention. If incommensurate intentions remain unreconciled, the world of personal agents will remain divided and at war with itself. This leads to the obvious conclusion that the freedom to satisfy one's intentions in a social order depends upon the freedom of all the others to do the same. The harmonious reconciliation of their freedoms is what Macmurray said we should call "community" (though he also means to include "society"). Unless the unity of the group is maintained, none of its members can satisfactorily achieve his or her intentions. And this fact leads to the development of a morality of action as the means to the end of social harmony.

MODES OF SOCIAL MORALITY

Macmurray believed that there are three typical modes of social morality, one based primarily on a positive apperception of the other (the communal mode), and the other two upon negative apperceptions (the pragmatic and the aesthetic). The positive mode of morality is heterocentric: to act for the other for the sake of the other. The other modes are negative and egocentric. They create an ideal world into which the self can, in imagination, escape in order to avoid the messy problems of direct encounters with the others.

The aesthetic mode of escape creates a spiritual world that is dualistically divided from the real world. The obligations of the self in the real world become of secondary value. The form of social life and morality that best corresponds to real world obligations is organic, "a system of social habit, in which the activity of each member is functionally related to the activity of the others, so that the practical life of the society is a balanced and harmonious unity, a system of social habit."[14] This leads to what Macmurray called the morality of "good form," an aesthetic of style, manners, tact, and grace. The real life of the self remains the life of withdrawal from this world, the life of contemplation.

The other negative mode of morality, the pragmatic, is the opposite of the aesthetic mode. It is the life of practical action in which the life of the spirit has become of secondary value. It is a morality of conflict and aggression, the securing of power to help me meet the threat I believe is posed by the presence and counter-intentions of hostile others who do not wish me well. Law becomes the primary expression of this kind of social relation because it provides restraint of and countervailing power to anyone seeking dominance of the others. This law can be both external and internalized (in the form of a sense of duty or social rules and principles for behavior).

COMMUNITY AND SOCIETY

This provides the transition for Macmurray into his all-important analysis of the relations between community and society. He often used the terms interchangeably up to this point and, in doing so, contributed to occasional confusion about some of the key concepts in his political philosophy.

He begins by noting that any human society is not only a fact; it must also be a matter of intention. The agents who make up human society must continuously will its unity if it is to survive (and without such a society there cannot be fulfillment of the person, who is by nature a social being). The unity of human society cannot, therefore, be exhaustively organic or aesthetic because organisms do not require the willing consent of their organs. The basis of any human society "is the universal and necessary intention to maintain the personal relation which makes the human individual a person, and his life a common life. It is the instantiation of the 'I and You' as the unit of the personal. It is constituted and maintained by loyalty and keeping faith."[15]

Not all societies require a state. Many societies are not essentially political (e.g., the bowling club, the PTA, the support group). The state emerges only when the society is large enough to have to deal with disproportionate impersonal exercises of power. The nation-state is a legal entity "whose limits are defined by the territorial boundaries of its legal authority."[16]

This requires the state to develop mechanisms for the exercise of power. In the pragmatic mode of morality, Hobbes provides a classic exposition of the state. The state (Leviathan) is the power that limits individual agents in order to ensure the harmony of the whole. "This alone," Macmurray argues, "can provide the sense of security which suppresses the fear of the Other and removes the necessity for self-defense. The power of government defends each individual against the self-interest of his neighbour."[17] (This presupposes, of course, the negative motivation of fear of the other for the sake of oneself.) Macmurray concludes that Hobbes's conception of society is one of atomic units, "inherently isolated or unrelated," held together by an external force that "counteracts the tendency of their individual energies to repel one another."[18] As rational beings, however, these units find it in their self-interest to willingly grant Leviathan this absolute power over their relational lives (provided its power does not intrude upon their private lives).

If his argument to this point has substance, then Macmurray's next move becomes natural. He argues that, in the long run, no society can flourish if the primary motivation of its members is negative: fear of the other. There has to be in human beings something that urges them toward a more fulfilling form of relationship. Hobbes puts too much weight upon reason and law to hold the society together. What Hobbes leaves out is what is found only in community: the natural desire of persons to enjoy being together with others for the sake of being together.

The other negatively motivated alternative to Hobbes is Rousseau, whose view of society is essentially organic. Macmurray argues that for Rousseau, human nature is naturally good but has been distorted by the social forms into which it has been forced.[19] The only form that is appropriate to human nature is organic because, by identifying our individual wills with the general will or the organic whole, we will both realize our intentions and secure the unity of the organism as a whole. Unlike Hobbes, Rousseau believes that private self-interest is not ultimately what we really want. We want to subordinate ourselves to the whole. Macmurray's criticism of this is that it substitutes an ideal, imaginary world (in which all wills are harmoniously united) for the real world in which they clearly are not. I can overcome the real conflict of wills by letting my will be determined by the general will, which on an organic model is bound to win out in the end because it is teleologically determined. In this organic Rousseauian society, Macmurray claims, "the only rational behaviour in practice is to submit to the Other, because whether I submit or resist makes no difference in the end. The Other is stronger than I, and will achieve its purpose in either case. . . . [I]f I struggle against the Other, I shall only make a lot of unpleasantness for myself and for other people, and I shall gain nothing by it."[20] When this is the case, the self is divided between a spectator self (the one which submits to the other) and a real self that escapes into an ideal world of the imagination. As spectator, the self lives in a social world but accepts its place there as a role to be played for the successful functioning of the organic whole. This reflects a negative conception of relationality. The members of the society "are isolated individuals, whose real life is private and separate; yet for each of them the protection of the society is necessary."[21] The inherent ideal of this kind of society is "an automatic harmony of wills produced by the suppression of self-interest in favour of the moral will for the general good" and in which I "mystically" identify myself with the whole of which I am a part.[22] The real self flourishes primarily in its private life (to which society is a means).

When the ideal harmony of the organic society breaks down (because it cannot consistently suppress self-interest), the state emerges, as it had in Hobbes, to maintain social unity. The problem with both the Hobbesian mechanical and the Rousseauian organic societies is their primarily negative forms of relationality. This is precisely what keeps them societies and not communities.

If we are going to be true to what Macmurray takes to be our underlying human nature, then we have to have forms of association that are more than societies. These, of course, are communities. They are "personal unities of persons as are based on a positive personal motivation [toward the Others]. The members of a community are in communion with one another, and their association is a fellowship . . . [which] exhibits the form of the personal in its fully positive personal character."[23] But as in any direct, personal relationship, the negative is never eliminated. A community "*will necessarily contain within it and be constituted by its own negative, which is society. Every community is then a society; but not every society is a community.*"[24]

The concept of community is the heart of Macmurray's political philosophy. It has been building in his thought almost from the very beginning.

While it receives reiteration in *Persons in Relation*, its essential ingredients were already prefigured in some detail in his work of less than a decade previous, *Conditions of Freedom*. Central to his understanding of community are the notions of heterocentricity, fellowship, friendship, freedom, equality, direct personal relations, objectivity, human nature, and the exclusion of no one, at least by intention, from the community. His understanding of politics and the state derives from and is dependent on his treatment of what he takes to be more basic to human nature, namely the conditions of fellowship in community.

HETEROCENTRICITY AND SELF-TRANSCENDENCE

Human nature is ultimately self-transcending. It seeks to realize itself only in and through a relationship with an objective other (or community of others). This is the basic and perhaps most audacious claim he makes: that we can only truly be ourselves through a self-transcendence that puts us into direct personal relations of love heterocentrically oriented toward personal others. (Love must be the dominant motive in these relationships, subordinating, but never eliminating, the motive of fear.) Only in relations of trust with the other can we "really be ourselves," Macmurray asserts.[25] "Only another person can elicit a total response in action, of such a kind that the self-transcendence of every aspect and element of our nature is expressed and fulfilled. This is the implicit intention of all fellowship—the complete realization of the self through a complete self-transcendence."[26] In other words, it is the essence of our human nature to live in terms of the objective reality of the others with whom we are in relation (in varying ways). The alternative is to live within ourselves. However, the fullness of the person cannot be found by going inward but only by going outward heterocentrically toward the others that the real world (the world of action) puts us in contact with daily.

Macmurray even suggests that the essence of rationality, as well as personality, is oriented to knowing the other objectively. If I want to be truly myself, I must live in terms of the other. When I do so, I will (ideally) achieve a "complete objectivity, complete rationality, a complete self-realization."[27] In the presence of the other whom I love heterocentrically, I can be free and spontaneous, unguarded, in short, truly myself without fear of rejection.

In its most extreme form, this heterocentricity entails, according to Macmurray, that "the other is the center of value. [The self] has no value in himself, but only for the Other; consequently he cares for himself only for the sake of the other."[28] Acting on this principle leads to the "ideal" of the personal as "a universal community of persons in which each cares for all the others and no one for himself."[29]

If one takes these incredible statements from within the mindset of an individualistic philosophy, they are absurd. They are self-negating, self-denying irrationalities. However, Macmurray would respond by reminding us that *individualism* as a philosophy is built on the Hobbesian notion that fear is the primary motive driving human political association. As long as we allow this negative (and always present) motive to dominate the motive of love, then the other is that of which we should be afraid. To love the other instead of ourselves would be, literally, absurd and irrational. But if human nature is such that it can only be fulfilled in relations of trust and love, *and assuming this is true for all those in relation*, then heterocentric orientation is rational. But conditions and qualifiers must be placed around Macmurray's assertions of heterocentricity.

The most important condition is that, for heterocentricity to work realistically, it must be intended by *all* the members in direct personal relationship with each other. It cannot be intended by only one member while all the rest pursue fearful, egotistical, individualistic motives. That would truly make heterocentricity irrational and absurd. But Macmurray carefully nuances his understanding of the heterocentric valuing of the other: "this is mutual. Each, that is to say, acts, and therefore thinks and feels for the other, and not for himself."[30] The essential condition, he says elsewhere, for *realizing* fellowship is a "mutual reciprocity. The individual cannot achieve freedom in fellowship unless the other person does so too. . . . Without reciprocity no common life can be established."[31]

This mutuality and reciprocity ensure that the individuals in relation are not submerged into each other, or into an organic whole in which they dissolve into being merely functional components. They remain genuinely different others to each other, bound in mutual love for each other. And they can give themselves to each other without fear of losing individuality because they have no overriding fear of the other or for themselves. Their unity, Macmurray insists, "is no fusion of selves, neither is it a functional unity of differences—neither an organic nor a mechanical unity—it is a unity of persons. Each remains a distinct individual; the other remains really other. Each realizes himself in and through the other. Such a positive unity of persons is the self-realization of the personal."[32]

Clearly this understanding of community does not require the annulment of the self or even a renunciation of its desire for self-fulfillment. Nor does it entail what some have taken to be the Christian position of extreme agape: one in which the self loves the other solely for the sake of the other because the self has no worth of its own (because of its sinfulness or depravity). In Macmurray's view all persons are of worth, and as long as one is the other to someone else, one's worth is respected, even loved by the others, as one is loving them reciprocally.

We should recall here as well the importance of Macmurray's notion of resistance. One cannot be a full self without resisting the overpowering smothering love of another. Part of what it means to be a full self is to be able to carve out one's own identity as a distinct individual. This is done by resisting the other up to a point (provided the resistance is the subordinated negative moment in an otherwise dominant positive orientation).

If the individuality of each is to be respected and upheld, other conditions are also necessary. One is the freedom of each in the relationship. Another is the equality of the partners. Freedom for the self occurs when the self can be itself without fear of the other. Thus fellowship is the "basic condition of freedom."[33] The equality of the partners in relation is mandatory if they are to enjoy each other instead of using each other. This equality is what they intend: it does not mean that they are equal with respect to such things as talent, skills, and so forth. Nevertheless they can be equal with respect to their ability to enter into direct, personal, loving relations with others. If the relationship itself was not between equals, then "the motivation would be negative; a relation in which one was using the other as a means to his own end."[34] Personal equality does not ignore natural differences nor the need for functional relations in a social order. Instead "it overrides them. It means that any two human beings, whatever their individual differences, can recognize and treat one another as equal, and so be friends."[35] The alternative is a master-slave relationship.

Freedom is also essential for friendship. If a "complete self-expression and self-revelation which is mutual and unconstrained" is of the essence of genuine friendship, then the partners cannot be afraid of freely expressing and revealing themselves. If fear is what restrains us from being fully ourselves in the presence of others, then only personal freedom can allow us to be ourselves in relationships with others. Friendship "provides the only conditions which release the whole of the self into activity and so enable a man to be himself totally, without constraint . . . freedom [therefore] is a constitutive principle of friendship."[36]

Macmurray warns us, however, that while constitutive of friendship, equality and freedom are never fully realized: they remain ideals and must be constantly *intended* by the partners in relation. Nevertheless, the more they are intended and acted upon, the more partial realizations of both will occur and each realization will contribute to the possibilities of further realization in the future.

POLITICAL IMPLICATIONS
OF THE FORM OF THE PERSONAL

At this point in his analysis, Macmurray's more specific political philosophy is engaged. If freedom and equality are constitutive of friendship and community, what is the role of the political or social order in their achievement and maintenance? Macmurray's central claim is that community cannot be a *political* objective or project, and the state cannot be its creator or administrator. The historical error of the West has been to confuse community with organized society and in the process set artificial territorial or national boundaries around fellowship. At the same time, the political approach to community has "endowed the political state with moral and spiritual qualities which imply its absoluteness, and contain the seeds of totalitarianism."[37] The state, he argues, can only provide the material conditions "in which fellowship can flourish and through which it can manifest itself."[38] Friendship is an end in itself and is enjoyed for its own sake. The state, at its best, develops mechanisms for cooperation for achieving common tasks. These may lead to friendship but they are not predicated on friendship. They are functional for the maintenance of the social order as a whole, not ends in themselves.

In "The Devices of Politics," a pivotal chapter in *Persons in Relation*, Macmurray brings his political philosophy to a succinct but crucial state of articulation. The state deals with persons in indirect relation with each other (the negative aspect of personal relationships). These relations constitute society as an intentional cooperative economic endeavor "directed upon the world-as-means, to the corporate production and distribution of the means of personal life in society."[39] These cooperative relations are functional relations through which each worker is identified with his or her function.

The economic work performed by persons in indirect relation with each other is pragmatic and is to be evaluated by its efficiency in delivering the goods. Obviously, no one labors just for the sake of producing goods: the goods themselves are justified as means to the living of a meaningful personal life. In this sense, economic activity is subordinate to the end that it serves: fellowship or community through which alone the person can be fully himself or herself.

Politics, it follows, is the "maintaining, improving and adjusting the indirect or economic relations of persons" in the social order.[40] Its institutional manifestation is the state and its primary function is the establishment and maintenance of justice.[41] For Macmurray, justice is the "minimum of reciprocity and interest in the other in the personal relation—what can rightly be exacted from him if it is refused . . . a kind of zero or lower limit of moral behaviour."[42] This is as true of direct, intimate, loving personal relationships as it is of indirect relationships in a cooperative society. A direct personal relationship that tries to go around justice, or ignore it, winds up creating conditions of inequality in the relationship and thus undermines its own reason for being. While justice is the negative element in a full personal relationship, it cannot be neglected, since the negative is always necessary to the constitution of the positive, though ideally subordinate to it.

Without justice, as Macmurray trenchantly puts it, morality "becomes illusory and sentimental."[43] Bypassing justice permits us to single out some others for special generous treatment and thus undermines the intentional inclusiveness of our reference to the other as a unity. It produces what Macmurray calls "a minor mutuality which is hostile to the interests of the larger community. It is to create and defend a corporate self-interest, and this destroys the universality of the moral reference. To be more than just to some and less than just to the others is to be unjust to all."[44]

Macmurray also reminds us that even in the most intimate direct personal relations, the negative aspect (justice) will be present even though it is subordinated to the positive (love). But unless justice is present, the two agents in relation may wind up being undifferentiated from each other. And this must not happen, because then the reciprocity of two individual persons will be lost and the "heterocentricity of the relation will be only apparent."[45] If freedom and equality are constitutive of fellowship, then justice serves to maintain them. Justice keeps one agent from becoming slavishly dependent on another. Justice preserves the differentiation and distinctness of persons that are essential for healthy direct personal relations. Justice limits the activities of all in relation to all so that each may enjoy the widest range of freedom possible within a cooperative endeavor. The only thing justice cannot do is actually *create* direct personal relations. That takes the intentionality of persons for community as an end in itself.

In a society, Macmurray argues, we need a "common consent to general principles" based on a sense of fairness. (The comparison to Rawls's notion of justice as fairness will be explored later.) This "contract" is a pragmatic device that intends to provide justice and combat injustice. (If we can't trust each other enough to abide by the contract, further devices will be necessary to provide pragmatic security.) Any government will ultimately rest upon the "universal and necessary intention to maintain social co-operation," without which there can be no politics. Politics depends on the "habit of co-operation in society."[46] This habit, Macmurray argues, begins to be developed in the family, which is, as he reminds us, the first community of persons from which society developed as familial relations became more extensive and less direct. Therefore, he says, "the state depends upon society and society depends upon community."[47] When the community of direct personal relations either breaks down or becomes too extensive to permit each and every member to have direct personal relations with all the other members, then the necessity for the state and politics arises.[48]

While justice is present even in direct personal relations, when the nexus of relationship becomes indirect, the "mechanism" of law will arise, which "will automatically adjust the relations between the individuals concerned in such a fashion that the activities of each do not injure the others."[49] Law provides the "minimum of interference with the practical freedom of the individual which is necessary to keep the peace."[50] It is "the means to justice in the indirect relations of persons co-operating for the production and distribution of the means of personal life."[51] The state is the pragmatic instrument for enforcing the law. It has no intrinsic value and is not an end in itself. Complex societies cannot do without the state insofar as "the necessary co-operation in society requires an adjustment of indirect human relations."[52] The state is a necessary device for any social life beyond a primitive state. Justice is necessary for social cooperation, law is necessary for justice, and the power of enforcement is necessary for law. The problem is to see that the devices of politics and the state are used only for the purposes for which they are intended. If the state does not succeed in maintaining a sense of justice among the members of the society, then it fails in its task and should be reformed or overthrown. Signs of its failure, according to Macmurray, are a lack of common consent to general principles of justice, serious complaints about unfairness, a lack of peace among the members, and a breakdown in the habits of cooperation.

Macmurray makes the point that obedience to the law can only be superceded by a higher moral obligation. Normally, we have a moral obligation to respect and maintain the law as the necessary instrument for justice. I have an obligation in particular to subordinate my personal interests to the interests of the whole society under a general principle that is the same for all like cases.[53]

Ideally (though probably never fully in practice) justice will characterize the indirect relations of persons in society. If this ideal should ever be reached, however, Macmurray believes that something in personal life will still be missing. If justice is the negative aspect of personal relationships, then the positive aspect will ultimately be sought by persons. They will discover that they can only be fulfilled as persons in those relationships that constitute the celebration and enjoyment of community. In short, society is for the sake of community, and community realizes what can only be hinted at in the necessary but always incomplete experience of social cooperation.

So we are back again to Kymlicka's initial question: "What more, or what else, is needed to sustain unity than shared political principles? This is one of the great unresolved questions of contemporary political philosophy."[54] Macmurray has now given his answer: community, friendship, or fellowship goes beyond without eliminating shared political principles.

NOTES

1. John Macmurray, *Persons in Relation* (New York: Harper and Brothers, 1961); reprinted, with an introduction by Frank G. Kirkpatrick (London: Humanities Press International, 1991), 17.

2. Macmurray, *Persons in Relation*, 48. Macmurray does note that a man can serve the role of the mother, though he doesn't develop the implications of this observation.

3. Macmurray, *Persons in Relation*, 61.

4. Macmurray, *Persons in Relation*, 69.

5. Macmurray, *Persons in Relation*, 70.

6. Macmurray, *Persons in Relation*, 72.

7. Macmurray, *Persons in Relation*, 74.

8. Macmurray, *Persons in Relation*, 81.

9. The language of "I-You" and "I-it" is remarkably close to that of Martin Buber. Macmurray once met Buber, who said "I see no difference between us. It is simply that you are the metaphysician and I am the poet." Quoted in Costello, *John Macmurray: A Biography* (Edinburgh: Floris Books, 2002), 322.

10. Macmurray, *Persons in Relation*, 82. Macmurray believed that organic objects were "persistently ambiguous" in terms of how they are to be discriminated. They fall somewhere between the purely mental and the purely material and can be discriminated only in practical terms. (*Persons in Relation*, 83.) The relation of material or mechanical dimensions of reality and the organic and personal dimensions was originally developed by Macmurray in *Interpreting the Universe*.

11. Macmurray, *Persons in Relation*, 91.

12. Macmurray, *Persons in Relation*, 78, 109.

13. Macmurray, *Persons in Relation*, 155.

14. Macmurray, *Persons in Relation*, 124.

15. Macmurray, *Persons in Relation*, 128.

16. Macmurray, *Persons in Relation*, 131.

17. Macmurray, *Persons in Relation*, 136.

18. Macmurray, *Persons in Relation*, 137.

19. It is not clear that Macmurray is being fair to Rousseau here.

20. Macmurray, *Persons in Relation*, 142.

21. Macmurray, *Persons in Relation*, 142.

22. Macmurray, *Persons in Relation*, 143.

23. Macmurray, *Persons in Relation*, 146.

24. Macmurray, *Persons in Relation*, 146. The emphasis is mine.

25. Macmurray, *Persons in Relation*, 150.

26. Macmurray, *Conditions of Freedom* (London: Faber and Faber, 1950), 82.

27. Macmurray, *Conditions of Freedom*, 82. It is rational because the essence of thought is to refer beyond itself to something other than itself.

28. Macmurray, *Persons in Relation*, 158.

29. Macmurray, *Persons in Relation*, 159.

30. Macmurray, *Persons in Relation*, 158.

31. Macmurray, *Conditions of Freedom*, 82–83.

32. Macmurray, *Persons in Relation*, 158.

33. Macmurray, *Conditions of Freedom*, 82.

34. Macmurray, *Persons in Relation*, 158.

35. Macmurray, *Conditions of Freedom*, 73.

36. Macmurray, *Conditions of Freedom*, 73.

37. Macmurray, *Conditions of Freedom*, 75.

38. Macmurray, *Conditions of Freedom*, 75.

39. Macmurray, *Persons in Relation*, 186.

40. Macmurray, *Persons in Relation*, 188.

41. Macmurray, *Persons in Relation*, 188.

42. Macmurray, *Persons in Relation*, 188.

43. Macmurray, *Persons in Relation*, 188–89.

44. Macmurray, *Persons in Relation*, 189.

45. Macmurray, *Persons in Relation*, 189.

46. Macmurray, *Persons in Relation*, 191.

47. Macmurray, *Persons in Relation*, 192.

48. Macmurray, *Persons in Relation*, 192.

49. Macmurray, *Persons in Relation*, 194.

50. Macmurray, *Persons in Relation*, 194.

51. Macmurray, *Persons in Relation*, 194.

52. Macmurray, *Persons in Relation*, 199.

53. Macmurray, *Persons in Relation*, 197.

54. Will Kymlicka, *Contemporary Political Philosophy*, 2nd ed. (Oxford: Oxford University Press, 2002), 257.

8

MACMURRAY AND
CONTEMPORARY
POLITICAL PHILOSOPHY

Macmurray's political philosophy does not easily fit into most categories of contemporary political philosophy. He is neither a strict liberal nor, despite his emphasis on community, a communitarian. He has a strong defense of the family but not necessarily the one that has been idealized by neoconservatives preaching "family values." He emphasizes love but at the same time insists on justice in even the most intimate of relationships. His views also track very closely those of the psychological school of object-relations theory in which broken relationships and their restoration have come to replace Freudian notions.

He has much to contribute to feminist thought but also is vulnerable to its critique on some points. He is strongly committed to the use of reason in philosophical analysis but also has a crucial place for the role of emotions in the complex web of human relationships. He is sympathetic to a national sense of identity while at the same time urging a more inclusive global society. He has influenced the New Labour politics of Tony Blair but might distance himself from some of the policies Blair has advocated.

MACMURRAY AND COMMUNITARIANISM

To begin with the obvious question: why is Macmurray not a full-fledged communitarian, given his strong emphasis on community as the locus for the fulfillment of the human person? The short answer is that the communitarians tend to confuse "society" with "community" and apply the latter term to a wide variety of political arrangements of persons without appreciating the differences between political societies and mutual communities.

The longer answer is that the treatment of society as community by many communitarians tends to embed the person too tightly in the bonds of a social arrangement (constrained and shaped by a particular tradition) that threatens personal autonomy. The "community" valorized by many communitarians does not allow enough individual freedom for persons to challenge the structures of their given society (which for Macmurray are essentially determined by the negative motivation of fear). Michael Sandel may be right in observing that every human person is "encumbered" to some degree by his or her location within a historically constructed social environment. In Sandel's view, the liberal, extolling free choice, lacks "the possibility of membership in any community bound by moral ties antecedent to choice; he cannot belong to any community where the self *itself* could be at stake. Such a community—call it constitutive as against merely cooperative—would engage the identity as well as the interests of the participants, and so implicate its members in a citizenship more thorough-going than the unencumbered self can know."[1]

The question Macmurray would ask is *how* thoroughgoing is this "implication"? Communitarian Alasdair McIntyre insists that we cannot escape being the "bearers of a particular social identity. . . . The story of my life is always embedded in the story of those communities from which I derive my identity."[2] But surely we have the freedom to question this embeddedness: we cannot be simply its passive prisoners.

Will Kymlicka argues that no matter how much we may inherit from the societies into which we are born and initially acculturated, "we *can* be mistaken about even our most fundamental interests, and because some goals *are* more worthy than others. Liberty is needed precisely to find out what is valuable in life—to question, re-examine, and revise our beliefs about value."[3] It is because our life-plans are so important that "we should be free to revise and reject them, should we come to believe that they are not fulfilling or worthwhile. . . . Freedom of choice [is] a precondition for pursuing those projects and tasks that *are* valued for their own sake."[4] It is not clear that communitarianism provides for the requisite freedom of choice to do this. And, as we have seen, the concept of individual freedom is a central notion in Macmurray's political philosophy.

Macmurray would agree with much of Derek Phillips's criticism of many communitarian claims. Phillips argues that many communitarians are uncritically supportive of some historical societies that were undemocratic, oppressive, and unjust to the poor and disenfranchised. He argues that the historical instances of community cited by the communitarians failed in almost every instance to embody the ideal image the communitarians project for them. Many of these "communities" achieved their unity at the expense of marginalizing diversity and restricting individual freedom, especially among those persons who did not belong to the communities' white male ruling elites.

Phillips also agrees with Kymlicka's claim that too much community can overwhelm or suppress individual rights, including the freedom to dissent both from what one takes to be oppressive structures of injustice and from the traditions that have shaped those particular "communities." The fact that persons seem to have their identity given to them (rather than chosen by them) only through their functional roles in a tightly bound and historically structured society suggests one of the most profound limitations in the communitarian philosophy. This limitation is precisely what Macmurray was attacking in his critique of the organic/functional view of society in which persons are reduced to their functional roles in maintaining the inclusive social organism of which they are merely the organs.

Phillips further critiques communitarianism for its vagueness in defining what it means by community. Its notion of community refers to nothing more substantive than "a group of people who live in a common territory, have a common history and shared values, participate together in various activities, and have a high degree of solidarity."[5] This hardly describes a community in Macmurray's sense and could equally well be applied to Stalinist Russia as to an Amish settlement, with no moral judgment about the relative worth of either. Communitarians often fail to provide any sense of what would constitute "good" or "just" communities and which ones must be judged as morally inferior because they have no underlying moral ontology.

Finally, Phillips notes that, despite their name, some communitarians' notion of community oddly leaves out what Macmurray would emphasize as central to real communities (though not necessarily to society): "regular face-to-face relations as an element in their conception of community."[6]

Because Macmurray grounds his political philosophy in a philosophy of the personal, he can lay down markers for any human society with respect to the social structures and policies it must enact if it is to be faithful to the conditions for human flourishing. These markers include justice, democracy, and the empowerment of voices of the previously marginalized and silenced, as well as individual freedom.

Part of what it means to be an individual in society is the right to define oneself as "an" individual, with a discrete identity that is not submerged in a group identity. This is where Macmurray's notion of resistance as an essential ingredient in the development of the self-in-relation is so important.

We are reminded of his claim that the child can only discover himself "as an individual by contrasting himself, and indeed willfully opposing himself to the family *to which he belongs*; and this *discovery* of his individuality is at the same time the *realization* of his individuality."[7] Action requires a resistance and, in the case of persons, a clash of wills.[8] And because persons are agents, individuality requires the resistance of the personal other. Unless the partners in the relation have differentiated themselves from each other, there will be no genuine relationship.[9] Communitarianism, to the extent that it leans toward an organic understanding of society in which the units (persons) are functional components subordinate to the whole of which they are merely contributing parts, tends to downplay the struggle for achieving individuality through resisting the imposition of wills upon the self. In this respect Macmurray is much closer to Kymlicka's and the liberal tradition's emphasis on the need for individual "space" in opposition to the society's will.

JOHN RAWLS AND THE LIBERAL POSITION

Despite his frequent invocation of the concept of community, Macmurray has more in common with liberalism than one might initially expect. John Rawls begins his famous book on justice with the assumption that society is "a system of cooperation designed to advance the good of those taking part in it. [It] is a cooperative venture for mutual advantage."[10] Macmurray would not quarrel with this definition of society, remembering that it is not identical with community.

The "original position" that Rawls invokes to establish the principles of justice would not, of course, apply in a community, but they do make sense for a society. As Rawls argues, the parties (behind a veil of ignorance as to their situations in real life) are driven primarily by self-interest. They have conflicting claims to the division of social advantages, they may have no extensive ties of natural sentiment, and they take no interest in one another's interests.[11] The parties have no reason to sacrifice any of their own interests in order that someone else's interests might be advanced over their own.[12] In this respect Rawls, at least in the original position, has to factor out any notion of love or heterocentrism among the parties.

Two principles emerge from the original position and constitute justice as fairness. The first principle is that "each person is to have an equal right to the most extensive basic liberty compatible with a similar liberty for others."[13] The second or difference principle holds that "social and economic inequalities are to be arranged so that they are both (a) to the greatest benefit of the least advantaged . . . and (b) attached to positions and offices open to all under conditions of fair equality and opportunity."[14]

As a liberal, Rawls maintains that there will be "conflicting and incommensurable conceptions of the good."[15] Individuals retain the right to choose their own life-plans by whatever criteria they adopt and not on the basis of any common, metaphysically grounded notion of what is good for all. As Rawls has famously said: "justice as fairness [is] the concept of right prior to that of the good."[16] This leads him to the view that the social principles that will "govern the background conditions under which" we make our individual choices of life-plans must be decided before we make decisions about what we value as good. "The self is prior to the ends which are affirmed by it."[17] The most we can hope for in a morally diverse society is an "overlapping consensus" as to what principles are to govern social life in order that individuals are given the greatest possible latitude to pursue their freely chosen individual life-plans.[18]

What Rawls has described is the form of a just *society*. It is the form of what Macmurray has called impersonal and usually indirect associations among persons each seeking his or her good under the conditions of the greatest possible degree of individual freedom and in accord with an overlapping consensus of general social principles. This is clearly a society rather than a community, in Macmurray's sense, since the latter presupposes a greater degree of direct personal relations, intimacy, mutual love, and a sense of being bound together by a common heterocentric commitment to seeking the good of all within it. Societies may provide the necessary material means and political conditions for smaller, more basic, more personally direct communities that can bring out in their members those qualities that lead to greater flourishing and fulfillment. Nevertheless, societies are not themselves communities, and communities do not require all the elements constitutive of societies. The crucial issue is the appropriate relation between communities and the societies in which they are embedded. The communitarian critics of liberalism would want to ask: does the free self-determining individual need any deeper form of community in which to flourish, or can life be lived to the fullest in and through the instrumentalities of formal justice and nothing more?

For the liberal, carrying forward the individualistic dimension of liberal political philosophy, the purpose of the state is simply to ensure that all citizens have equal opportunity to advance whatever conception of the good they might individually happen to hold, provided only that they do so without violating the initial two principles of justice. The only necessary conception of the person in the liberal society is a political one at the heart of which is the primacy of the individual's freedom to choose his or her own life-plan without unfair coercion by others. What Macmurray wants to raise is the question of whether there is, in fact, a sense of the flourishing person that locates his or her fulfillment more appropriately in some forms of community that go beyond or add to what those same persons find in a just society.

JUSTICE AND POLITICS

As we have seen earlier, politics, for Macmurray, is the "maintaining, improving and adjusting [of] the indirect or economic relations of persons."[19] The institutional expression of politics is the state, whose central function is to maintain justice. Justice, in this context, is the minimum of reciprocity and interest in the other in the personal relation: it is a "kind of zero or lower limit of moral behavior."[20] It keeps relationships from disintegrating under the centrifugal force of suspicion and animosity.

This view of justice comes very close to that of Rawls. While not requiring altruism or heterocentrism on the part of those in the original position, Rawls does presume enough common interest among them so that they can all agree on a set of principles that will bind them together in various forms of indirect impersonal relations of economic and political transactions. These relations constitute society.

As subordinate to mutuality, justice insists on differentiation between individuals in the social relation. Justice seeks to avoid the possibility that the partners will seek to submerge their individual identities in the needs and demands of the others for whom they are caring.[21] Justice keeps morality that is person-focused from becoming romantic or falling into what Macmurray calls "a minor mutuality" that is hostile to the justice interests of the larger society. Persons who focus exclusively on the intimacy of their relationship can easily block out the needs of others with whom they are not in such intimate relationship. If those others are impaired in their ability to flourish because the conditions under which they live are unjust, then the intimate lovers focused exclusively on themselves in their "minor mutuality" can contribute nothing to the pursuit of justice for the impaired. The other must remain other, both in society and in community, and justice attempts to see to it that this will be the case in both.

Justice also stands as a safeguard against the danger of a larger organic whole absorbing individuals without granting them the respect they are due because of their unique individualities. An organic form of social relationship in which there is a single common good and a single set of approved moral practices runs the risk of totalitarianism. Situating justice firmly within a communitarian "community," as a reminder that it is not the fullness of mutuality, keeps the latter from degenerating into a purely sentimental, or totalitarian whole in which the rights of the individual get swamped by the imperatives of group solidarity. Justice acts as a block on forms of organic social unity that privilege ethnic, gender, class, racial, or other types of identity to the exclusion of individual rights to make free choices about life-plans and the means to accomplish them.

PRESERVING PARTICULARITY AND OTHERNESS

Iris Marion Young has been particularly clear about warning of the danger of using the rhetoric of community to subordinate the uniqueness of individual persons to a group identity.[22] She is afraid that the "ideal" of community (which she consistently confuses with a concept of society) requires a "*fusion of subjects* [emphasis mine] with one another which in practice operates to exclude those with whom the group does not identify. The ideal of community denies and represses social difference . . . in its privileging of face-to-face relations."[23] Young's basic point is that when face-to-face relationships are privileged, politics, as the negotiation of differences, is avoided. When this happens, the structures of oppression remain unchallenged.[24]

Young's claim that community requires a fusion between the members completely misses Macmurray's argument for increasing differentiation (even resistance) between persons. Nevertheless, her insistence that even in close relationships justice must be present is a helpful reminder that community must not swallow the self in an organic whole to which it is subordinated or defined by its functionality.

Even the deepest friendships cannot pretend to have transcended the need for justice. To allow friends to be immune from the standards of justice can become an excuse for their abuse and exploitation. One partner in a relationship may bear a greater burden and derive less immediate benefit for her efforts than the other partner. "Justice," Marilyn Friedman notes, "sets a constraint on such relationships by calling for an appropriate sharing, among the participants, of the benefits and burdens that constitute their relationship."[25] Friedman argues that justice in personal relationships does not conflict with care or love, but does provide love with the necessary constraints, conditions, and resources to do its work without falling into abuse and effete sentimentalism. Justice is part of the way in which we can truly care for other persons. The bare minimum of that care is to "respect their rights and accord them their due, both in the distribution of the burdens and benefits of social cooperation and in the rectification of wrongs done."[26]

Macmurray would agree with this reminder precisely because, as he argues, "there must be no self-identification of the one with the other, or the reciprocity will be lost and the heterocentricity of the relation will be only apparent."[27] One of the ends of justice is to establish and maintain the equality of persons in their social and economic relations. Each agent must have freedom of action, without which he or she cannot be independent of the others.[28] This independence is, in a sense, the negative element in the positive relationship of *interdependence*. In a passage that has striking parallels with Rawls, Macmurray argues that "I can hope to secure justice in my dealings with [others] by limiting my activities for the sake of their interests, provided they will do the same in their dealings with me. . . . We can consult together and come to an agreement about what is fair to each of us, so far as our separate courses of action affect one another and impinge on one another. This can be achieved by a common consent to general principles by reference to which each of us can determine what would or would not be fair to the other person if we did it. Such agreement is a contract between us, which . . . determines reciprocal rights and obligations which we engage ourselves to respect. It is a pragmatic device to secure justice in cooperation and to eliminate injustice."[29]

Like Rawls, Macmurray assumes society is a cooperative endeavor based on a contractual understanding that protects the rights of individuals by limiting the activities of all for the sake of each. The parties to the contract must reach common consent (which is the purpose of the original position). Macmurray does not presume the veil of ignorance, but there is no reason to assume that he would be opposed to it as a heuristic device (which is the use to which Rawls puts it) because it ensures that the common consent will not unfairly privilege some at the expense of others.

INTERACTIVE COMMUNICATIVE ETHICS

Macmurray would also agree, however, with much of what has been called the communicative ethics position, in particular its criticism that Rawls's original position runs the risk of obscuring the uniqueness of the concrete other, the individual person who cannot be reduced to a general, purely rational self. Seyla Benhabib, a feminist moral philosopher drawing on the discourse ethics of Jürgen Habermas, calls this position "interactive universalism."[30] Like Macmurray, she holds out for some form of ontologically based universal moral principles. Her stance is pragmatic, based on the actual discourse of persons in interactive communication with each other in any particular form of human association. She agrees with the communitarians that the self is "embodied and embedded" with an identity that is narratively constituted. She also agrees with liberalism that the moral point of view is a contingent achievement, not a "timeless standpoint of a legislative reason"[31] (the Kantian factor). An interactive discourse ethic asks what principles of action participants engaged in practical discourse can agree upon.[32] This clearly tracks with both Rawls's and Macmurray's notion of persons consulting together to reach common consent about the principles of justice in a social order.

Consistent with her search for the universalization of moral principles, Benhabib rejects the extreme claims of cultural relativists who believe that there is nothing beyond the incommensurability of moral frameworks. If one is truly prepared to hear a different voice from one's own and to reformulate one's views as a result if the arguments are persuasive, then different moral positions can be debated constructively. There has been, Benhabib claims, more agreement between cultures about basic human values than the "armchair philosophers of cultural relativism" have been willing to acknowledge. In the process they have ignored the multiplicity of complex ways in which a common humanity can move from being an abstract ideal to becoming a concrete reality.[33] This last claim from a secular moral philosopher echoes Macmurray's theological claim in *The Clue to History* that God's intention for the unity of humankind is increasingly becoming a historical reality because it is the ontological basis for the fulfillment of humankind.[34]

Unlike strict liberals who insist that procedures determining the right are more basic and universal than any particular conceptions of the good chosen by individuals, Benhabib insists that communicative ethics entails strong normative assumptions about the moral status of persons within the communicative community. Among these are the "principle of universal moral respect" and the "principle of egalitarian reciprocity."[35] Both of these principles accord with Macmurray's notion of equality and the differentiation of the other as truly other in any genuine personal relationship. "We ought to *respect* each other as beings whose standpoint is worthy of equal consideration," Benhabib asserts, and "we ought to treat each other as concrete human beings whose capacity to express this standpoint we ought to enhance by creating, whenever possible, social practices embodying the discursive ideal (the principle of egalitarian reciprocity)."[36]

The second principle requires us to engage in what Benhabib calls the reversal of perspectives. We should be able to think from the other person's point of view and see how he or she judges others. Only if we do this can we avoid consigning others to a diminished status of otherness that would undermine their contribution to the interactive communicative conversation that constitutes the good society. This is especially true of those who have traditionally been excluded from the conversation, namely women and minorities.

In this regard Benhabib criticizes Rawls for ignoring the standpoint of the *concrete* other,[37] by subsuming him or her under "the disembedded and disembodied *generalized* other."[38] Behind the veil of ignorance "the *other as different from the self* disappears." The particular self is abstracted from his or her concrete and specific identity within the complex of human social relationships and treated simply as one of many indistinguishable selves. As a result, his or her voice as this different and unique other is effectively silenced. What remains is a self in general and no one in particular. To create the conditions for real community in which real persons are real contributors, the concrete, embedded lives of different concrete others must be included. This is what Macmurray calls the heterocentric dimension of relationship.

The inclusion of traditionally excluded particular others also undercuts the privileging of certain individualistic moral ideals, such as the abstract "economic man" as agent of rational choice. Benhabib argues that once the voices of women are brought into the conversation, morality as the rational actions of impersonal agents (traditionally white males) in a field of indirect relations, such as economics and politics, will be challenged. Employing the term that characterizes Macmurray's vision of community (but without any knowledge of that vision), Benhabib claims that communicative ethics "projects a utopian way of life in which *mutuality* [emphasis added], respect and reciprocity become the norm among humans as concrete selves and not just as juridical agents."[39] Macmurray's insistence that a heterocentric ethic focus on the uniqueness of the other, and not on his or her usefulness for the egocentric self or the social organism, suggests a similar support for treating others as concrete and not simply as generalized others.

EMPOWERING POSITIVE LIBERTY

Other thinkers today are echoing Macmurray's concern for providing the material support for the full human life. Macmurray had argued that the spiritual life (the life of love and mutuality) cannot be separated from its material base. "Without adequate material resources, the personal life must remain stunted and undeveloped. . . . The means of life are also the means of a good life."[40] Carol Gould similarly has argued that if the treatment of others in their concrete individuality is to be just, it must empower all the members of the society with the necessary material means, economic, social, and political, for the full exercise of one's personhood. This requires, in turn, "the availability of the objective conditions—both material and social—without which the purposes [of the self] could not be achieved."[41] Among these conditions are the means for daily subsistence, labor, leisure activity, and access to training and education.

If these conditions are met, Gould suggests, a sense of reciprocity or mutuality may begin to develop among the members of the society. People may come to share and adopt as their own the common purposes of the group to which they belong. They may choose to value the mutual support that individuals give to each other in the self-development of each.[42] Gould calls this relationship of mutual support "full reciprocity" or *mutuality*, which she defines as "a relation in which (a) each agent recognizes the other as free and as capable of self-development, (b) each acts with regard to the other in ways that enhance the other's self-development on the basis of a consideration of the other's needs, and (c) both agents take such mutual enhancement of each other's agency as a conscious aim."[43]

Another form of mutuality may also develop that is equally essential to self-development. "It consists in the contribution that is made . . . by all those individuals who, in the development of their own capacities, have enriched the range of possible human actions, intentions, skills, and practices. This cultivation of human capacities provides an individual with options or models for his or her own development."[44]

These forms of mutuality are not essential to political democracy, however. Only social reciprocity is required for that.[45] Mutuality, as Gould understands it, presumes "an altruism that is supererogatory" in a political context.[46] In this sense she seems to echo Macmurray's notion of heterocentricity as the essential element in community, as that which goes beyond society as such. What seems absent from both Benhabib's and Gould's use of the term "mutuality," however, is Macmurray's sense of the intrinsic delight of fellowship and love among persons for whom community is an end in itself, not simply a means to self-fulfillment.

NOTES

1. Michael Sandel, "The Procedural Republic and the Unencumbered Self," in *Communitarianism and Individualism*, ed. Shlomo Avineri and Avner De-Shalit (New York: Oxford University Press, 1992), 19.

2. Alasdair MacIntyre, *After Virtue* (Notre Dame, Ind.: University of Notre Dame Press, 1981), 205.

3. Will Kymlicka, "Liberalism and Communitarianism," *Canadian Journal of Philosophy* 18 (June 1988): 185.

4. Kymlicka, "Liberalism and Communitarianism," 187.

5. Derek L. Phillips, *Looking Backward: A Critical Appraisal of Communitarian Thought* (Princeton, N.J.: Princeton University Press, 1993), 14.

6. Phillips, *Looking Backward*, 15.

7. John Macmurray, *Persons in Relation* (New York: Harper and Brothers, 1961); reprinted, with an introduction by Frank G. Kirkpatrick (London: Humanities Press International, 1991), 91.

8. John Macmurray, *The Self as Agent* (London: Faber and Faber, 1957); reprinted, with an introduction by Stanley M. Harrison (London: Humanities Press International, 1991), 145.

9. This claim qualifies some of the more extreme statements of some Christian theologians (e.g., Anders Nygren) that would contrast *agape* love and *eros* love. Agape love, in this construal, loves the other as other because it is literally worthless (the paradigm example is God's love for corrupt humanity). But as Gene Outka and others have pointed out, love given to or received by a worthless being is itself worthless. Both partners in the relationship need to have some worth in order for their mutual love to be meaningful.

10. John Rawls, *A Theory of Justice* (Cambridge, Mass.: Harvard University Press, 1971), 4.

11. Rawls, *A Theory of Justice*, 127–29.

12. Rawls, *A Theory of Justice*, 14. In this respect Rawls qualifies traditional utilitarian theory.

13. Rawls, *A Theory of Justice*, 60–61.

14. Rawls, *A Theory of Justice*, 302.

15. John Rawls, "Justice as Fairness: Political not Metaphysical," *Philosophy and Public Affairs* 14 (1985): 245.

16. Rawls, *A Theory of Justice*, 31.

17. Rawls, *A Theory of Justice*, 560.

18. John Rawls, "The Priority of Rights and Ideas of the Good," *Philosophy and Public Affairs* 17 (1988): 252.

19. Macmurray, *Persons in Relation*, 188.

20. Macmurray, *Persons in Relation*, 188.

21. This is the fear that philosophers like Marilyn Friedman have about too much emphasis on care as a basis for morality. See, for example, her "Care and Context in Moral Reasoning," in *What Are Friends For? Feminist Perspectives on Personal Relationships and Moral Theory* (Ithaca, N.Y.: Cornell University Press, 1993).

22. Iris Marion Young, "City Life and Difference," *Justice and the Politics of Difference* (Princeton, N.J.: Princeton University Press, 1990).

23. Young, "City Life and Difference," 227.

24. Young, "City Life and Difference," 234.

25. Marilyn Friedman, "Gendered Morality," in *What Are Friends For?* 129.

26. Friedman, "Gendered Morality," 135.

27. Macmurray, *Persons in Relation*, 189.

28. Macmurray, *Persons in Relation*, 190.

29. Macmurray, *Persons in Relation*, 191.

30. Seyla Benhabib, *Situating the Self* (New York: Routledge, 1992), passim.

31. Benhabib, *Situating the Self*, 6.

32. Benhabib, *Situating the Self*, 28.

33. Benhabib, *Situating the Self*, 62–63, note 48.

34. Macmurray argues in *The Clue to History* (London: SCM Press, 1938), that "human intentions which are opposed to the intention of God for man are necessarily self-frustrating" (94–95). This means that "there are limits to the length that men can go on frustrating their own nature" (96).

35. Benhabib, *Situating the Self*, 29.

36. Benhabib, *Situating the Self*, 31.

37. Benhabib, *Situating the Self*, 161.

38. Benhabib, *Situating the Self*, 160.

39. Benhabib, *Situating the Self*, 60, note 34.

40. John Macmurray, *Constructive Democracy*, 21–22.

41. See Carol Gould, *Rethinking Democracy: Freedom and Social Cooperation in Politics, Economy, and Society* (Cambridge: Cambridge University Press, 1988), 39–41.

42. Gould, *Rethinking Democracy*, 50.

43. Gould, *Rethinking Democracy*, 77.

44. Gould, *Rethinking Democracy*, 50.

45. Gould, *Rethinking Democracy*, 77.

46. Gould, *Rethinking Democracy*, 292.

9

THE FAMILY AND
SMALL COMMUNITIES
IN POLITICAL THOUGHT

For all that the family has been valorized, idealized, and exploited for political purposes, it remains for many political philosophers an extremely important "community" necessary both for the development of personhood and for nurturing values and virtues contributory to a robust democratic political life. Macmurray has provided a central place in his political philosophy for the family. A similar place for family and smaller communities within a larger liberal society has actually been recognized by many liberal political philosophers, including John Rawls. As Roberto Alejandro has pointed out, Rawls has acknowledged the importance of smaller communities, or what he calls "social unions" within the larger society. As a result he accepts a version of an "encumbered self" who attains fulfillment as a person only in one form of community or another.[1] Rawls admits that "there should be for each person at least one community of shared interests to which he belongs and where he finds his endeavors confirmed by his associates."[2] This notion of communal confirmation suggests that, even for Rawls, persons do not fully flourish outside of some kind of communal context, smaller than the society as a whole, where they are affirmed and appreciated by others. A person depends on others "to confirm his sense of his own worth."[3] Rawls admits that "only in social union is the individual complete."[4] This suggests that Rawls understands that society as such is not sufficient for the completion of the deepest aspirations of human beings. They require closer, more direct, and personal forms of community, and this fact opens Rawls up to a consideration of communal relationships that go beyond, without replacing, societal principles of justice.

Carried even further, one can agree with David Wong's observation that liberal neutrality with respect to conceptions of the good may need to be compromised "because promoting community means promoting some conceptions of the good over others. It means favoring those conceptions that accord a high value to community itself [as Rawls obviously does in this section of his work]. Moreover, promoting and sustaining particular communities would seem to favor the conceptions of the good that these communities embody and that serve as part of their unifying basis."[5]

If this is true, Alejandro is right in claiming that "a Rawlsian community is far from being a mere attribute . . . it is *constitutive* [emphasis added] of the individual's identity," just as the communitarians claim.[6] What Rawls does not do is argue that any *one particular kind* of community or social union is better than another. But clearly the family constitutes one particular kind of community in and through which persons experience the delights of community even as they are being prepared for their work in society.

OBJECT-RELATIONS THEORY

One of the most important confirmations of Macmurray's claim that personal relationships, especially the family, are at the heart of human well-being and fulfillment has come from within the field of psychology, particularly from what is called object-relations theory. W. R. D. Fairbairn, one of its earliest proponents, states the fundamental conviction of object-relations theory: "A relationship with an object and not the gratification of an impulse" is the ultimate aim of human beings.[7] Fairbairn maintains that "human experience and behavior derive fundamentally from the search for and maintenance of contacts with others"[8] who are real persons, not ideas or images. The psychological task, therefore, is to deal with the "disturbances and interferences in relations with others" by helping the patient develop or restore a "capacity for making direct and full contact with real other human beings." For Fairbairn, as for Macmurray, this means that "the crucial aspect of healthy maturity is a capacity for a rich and intimate mutuality with another."[9] The goal of the therapeutic process is the restoration of full mutuality in personal relations. "If relations with others were nonproblematic, if satisfying contacts could be established and maintained, psychology would consist simply of the study of the individual's relations with other people."[10]

Fairbairn and other object-relations theorists trace (as does Macmurray) disruption in relationships back to childhood. If the child's relation to its mother[11] is a bad one (due to deprivation of appropriate affection and caring), the child compensates by creating "internal objects inside himself, which act as substitutes and solutions for unsatisfying relationships with real external objects."[12]

The primary experience of deprivation is that of an unavailable, unresponsive parent. The child can overcome this experience of failed relationships only when he can give up the fantasy of having total control of his internal objects. D. W. Winnicott suggests that the healthy relations are restored when the child learns to accept the "limits of his powers and becomes aware of the independent existence of others" who presumably are not controllable in the same way the self is.[13] The place in which this restoration of relations ought to occur is the family because it is often the place from which the disruption of relationality first began.

Again, consistent with Macmurray's work in *Persons in Relation*, object-relations theory maintains that fear is the negative that must be overcome. Through therapy, the patient may be able to come to a stronger sense of self that grows beyond "paralyzing fear or guilt." Object-relations theory, extended beyond the family, also suggests the indispensability of mutual community for complete fulfillment and health.

Ultimately what must be achieved is a "mature dependence" on others, which recognizes the need for relationships with them but is not servile or infantile. This involves, according to Fairbairn, a process of moving from infantile dependence to "a capacity for adult mutuality."[14] This form of mature mutuality accepts interdependence as a necessary element in healthy relationships and contains both a sense of individual identity and what Macmurray would call a heterocentric orientation toward the welfare of others.

Feminist writers have seen the virtue of object-relations theory for helping avoid an undue emphasis on the rational, autonomous, self-sufficient, independent self. As Nancy Chodrow has argued, object-relations makes clear that "the core of the self . . . is constructed relationally."[15] Like Macmurray, she also maintains, along with object-relations theory, that if the self is "constructed in a relational matrix," it can "better recognize the other as a self and, ultimately, attain the intersubjectivity that creates society."[16]

Another object-relations theorist, Harry Guntrip (a student of Macmurray's), maintains that with the right kind of support in the context of a loving community, the healthy person will be free to form significant personal relationships "in which there is a genuine meeting of kindred spirits . . . and to exercise an active and spontaneous personality free from inhibiting fears."[17]

The family can be the loving community that, under the right enabling conditions, provides exactly the right support to help children become healthy, mature, interdependent, relational selves. And if this is the case, then one of the most important tasks for the devices of politics is to enable families to flourish and to provide them the kind of empowering material support to which both Gould and Macmurray point.

Carol Gilligan has observed that the dispositions toward both justice and caring "arise from the experience of inequality and attachment embedded in the relationship between child and parent."[18] But the image of the self having the capacity for compassionate engagement with others, while clearly present in child development, is not adequately represented in political conceptions of the self as autonomous and individualistic. A stress on justice and autonomy, she argues, "impl[ies] a view of the individual as separate and of relationships as either hierarchical or contractual, bound by the alternatives of constraint and cooperation." "Women's thinking," by contrast, implies a view of the self and other "as interdependent and of relationships as networks created and sustained by attention and response."[19] Dependence on others, in this perspective, indicates that one is genuinely open to being moved by others and to responding to them in return. "Being dependent . . . no longer means being helpless, powerless and without control; rather it signifies a conviction that one is able to have an effect upon others, as well as the recognition that the interdependence of attachment empowers both the self and the other, not one at the other's expense."[20] This suggests the crucial importance of inclusive interactive dialogue, just as Benhabib and Macmurray have insisted, as the core of relationality. "The self is defined by gaining perspective and known by experiencing engagement with others."[21]

Where does the experience of relationality and differentiation of persons into individual selves in a mode of interdependence begin? The family is the core of this experience and its healthy development. (Or at least it can be: in developing a model of the family, one is setting forth a normative conception against which false and unhealthy models can be compared and found wanting.)

Susan Moller Okin has said, "the family is the primary institution of formative moral development. And the structure and practices of the family must parallel those of the larger society if the sense of justice is to be fostered and maintained."[22] Okin reminds us that this is where Rawls's work is so significant for women. His original position forces us to think about what is good for all persons in society without knowing ahead of time whether we are women or men, black or white, advantaged or disadvantaged. The problem with the communitarian alternative to this kind of liberalism is that it builds on "prevailing ideologies of male elites, and [thus] lack[s] moral force because their neglect of domination leaves the rest of us deprived of a voice in the construction of morality."[23]

Jean Bethke Elshtain has rightly said that "the family is the linchpin in all visions of future alternatives."[24] She claims that "some form of familial existence is a presuppositional feature of social existence" and that one must "articulate a *particular ideal* of family life that does not repeat the earlier terms of female oppression and exploitation."[25] No matter how oppressive families can be in practice, the idea of the healthy development of a child outside the context of familial nurture, care, love, and trust is virtually inconceivable. Elshtain says (in parallel with object-relations theory) that if children suffer in early childhood from neglect and nonattachment, they will "incur an assault to their humanness." In the properly constructed family, we are "dealing with a categorical imperative of human existence."[26] If this is the case, Elshtain continues, in a way that reinforces both Gould and Macmurray, the political task is to focus our energies on the political and economic structures that presently, in many forms of capitalist society, impede the work of the family in helping it to sustain "rich, long-lasting, cross-generational ties."[27] It is not the family that should be the target of feminist criticisms but the institutional and structural arrangements that make it impossible for parents, especially mothers, to attend to the work of nurturing and fostering the bonds of affection and mutuality within the family. "The heart of 'politics and the family' should lie . . . in fighting the pressures at work from the outside which erode, impoverish, or preclude the flourishing of our most basic human ties."[28] This does not mean, of course, the submersion of the individual family member into an organic whole called "the family." Elshtain would remind us, in a way that is clearly consistent with Macmurray, that "efforts can and should be made to take the edge off the predatory aspects of individualism, but to sacrifice the concept of the *individual* is to guarantee in advance the failure of one's reconstructive ideal and to invite unchecked political terror. . . . [I]t is the individual who is the basic unit of action even as the ideal of politics is a participatory one."[29]

One of the most important ingredients in a healthy family is building up the capacity to trust and diminishing the tendency to fear the others with whom one is in relationship. Fear, Macmurray holds, is the most important obstacle to establishing relations of trust, intimacy, mutuality, and love. Trust is the basis, in turn, for the capacity of heterocentrism.

Trust is an essential part of any fulfilling mutual relationship that contributes to human flourishing. Being in a truly interdependent relationship "presupposes a substantial degree of trust."[30] The moral philosopher Laurence Thomas links the presence of trust to altruism, or, in Macmurray's terms, heterocentrism. Thomas argues that the trust involved in caring relationships substantiates the altruism of parental love as "the most basic and generally the richest expression of altruism among human beings."[31] Parents are usually the people who, in Robert Adams's words, "not only had the concept of our good before we did, but also cared about our good before we could even conceive it."[32]

This example of parental heterocentrism suggests to Thomas that "there has to be more altruism in our bones . . . than contemporary moral philosophers have allowed."[33] Thomas also claims that "individuals who do not have their altruistic motivations manifestly realized in their lives flourish less than those who do."[34] The most important practice of altruism, what he calls "transparent" love, is found, as object-relations theory also suggests, in the original parent–child relationship. This "is unconditional love . . . because there is no belief about that individual's behavior, performances, or what have you, that constitutes a conceptual bar to so loving that person. There is nothing a person can do, nothing a person can become, that would cause one, on conceptual grounds, to cease loving him."[35] If parental love (taking the child's well-being "to heart, to delight in her flourishing") is unstinting, it is not a mystery why the child "comes to be disposed to forgo a benefit for the sake of others, since in this regard *fear no longer plays the explanatory role* [emphasis mine]"[36] in how the child learns to be loving in turn. The elimination (or at least subordination) of fear is the necessary prerequisite to genuine love of the other, just as Macmurray had argued. Fear, Thomas argues, "need not be a motivating factor in the life of the child. [Rather] it is out of love for and admiration of the parents that the child is motivated to comply with their wishes and to adopt their values."[37] This suggests that Macmurray was right to focus upon the development of the individual from within the context of a loving family and only as an extension of this to study how personal loving relationships (positively motivated with the negative element of fear and distrust subordinated) eventually have to be modified as persons begin to relate to each other politically and economically in less direct, less personal ways in society.

But this puts an enormous burden on the family to "get it right" from the very beginning. What the family clearly doesn't need are additional burdens laid on by unjust social structures and assumptions about the roles of men and women, husbands and wives, mothers and fathers. It is crucial that, as one moves from the private sphere of the family to the social sphere of the society, one does not ignore the crucial role of justice *within* the family, as Elshtain, Okin, Wong, and others have clearly argued.

Macmurray himself was quite clear that the family is a social construction of a sort. Marriage and the family exist, he argues, for the sake of the personal life. And while it may be true that monogamous marriage is the best social form for the relation between men and women, this cannot be taken for granted across all societies. The test of social forms is "their effect upon the freedom that is fundamental to the moral life of personality."[38] He even says that the test of a family is pragmatic. A social institution can be "justified if it makes possible the equality and freedom of human beings in the personal life." To maintain marriage or the family primarily by legal or economic pressure is unjustified. The real task is "to seek out and get rid of the obstacles which prevent equality and freedom from existing in the relationships of men and women to each other."[39]

In a piece entitled "Conditions of Marriage Today," Macmurray said that "the family is now too small a unit for the burdens it is expected . . . to carry. . . . Listening to the siren call of the economist for greater mobility of labour" makes the nuclear family insufficient.[40] If it is to survive at all, it can only be in the context of a wider sense of community and society. In the case of the latter, major structural changes will be needed that do not put undue stress on mothers rather than fathers, and even parents alone rather than also communally based support instrumentalities.

The relationships that constitute marriage are, for Macmurray, rooted in the practice of treating each other as individuals and celebrating the differences between us "as the means for realizing and expressing and enjoying our common personality."[41] At the heart of these relationships is emotional sincerity, or what he calls "chastity." This simply means expressing what you feel freely, without fear, to the other person with whom you are in relationship. If there is emotional sincerity, sex is appropriate, even with someone who is not one's spouse. If there is no emotional sincerity, sex is inappropriate even with one's spouse. Only "real personal love is the basis in the absence of which specifically sexual relations are unchaste and immoral."[42]

This belief was tested by Macmurray's own relationship with his wife, Betty. Sometime in the late 1920s, she confessed to him that she was having a sexual affair with another man. While initially devastated, Macmurray came to accept her decision when she explained that with her lover she was experiencing a degree of physical passion she had not known during her strict Scottish Calvinist upbringing. She expressed her feelings about this passion with what he would call "emotional sincerity" and said it did not diminish her feelings of love toward him in any way. Significantly, Betty used John's own notion of resistance to justify her actions. As John Costello puts it: "she reminded him of his own view that children become mature individuals by 'resisting' their given circumstances, by risking expressing their own desire in action. . . . And she recalled for him the central place he gave

to trust in any genuine, free relationship. She was asking him for that trust."
Eventually, according to Costello, they both accepted what would today be
called an "open" marriage in which they affirmed that "their friendship and
their marriage was the absolute relationship in their lives and that no other
relationship would be allowed to threaten it. . . . They promised with regard
to other sexual partners to be open with one another, and to foster in their
marriage whatever would promise to deepen their own love and friendship."[43]

In her otherwise appreciative commentary on Macmurray's work,
Christian feminist Susan Parsons has taken him to task precisely for his
notion of resistance as it pertains to the mother in the family relationship.
Parsons argues that the mother is presented by Macmurray from a male
perspective as the one who helps her son become a man through her role
as the shatterer of the boy's fantasies of complete satisfaction: she is to
"cause, to bring about this disillusionment, for she is to 'challenge,' to 'resist,' to 'govern,' and finally deliberately to 'refuse' his demands so that he
may grow up to be fully human." Parsons is referring to Macmurray's
words in *Persons in Relation* when he says that the crucial decision in the
child's development "rests with the mother, and therefore it must take the
form of a deliberate refusal on her part to continue to show the child
those expressions of her care for him that he expects."[44] Because Macmurray tends to see the mother only in her role, she disappears as a person in her own right. If mutuality is genuine, then it is not clear that the
mother–child relation is mutual, since the mother "is not fully present as
herself at all," nor is there an adequate treatment of the adult relationship
of man and woman.[45]

I think Parsons is too harsh on Macmurray here. She has failed to con-
textualize his discussion of the mother–child relationship (which clearly extends to female children as well as male). As we have seen, Macmurray elsewhere in his work treats the mother as a complete person in various kinds
of relationships. He even suggests that the "mother" is a stand-in for any
parent who is involved in the child's development. Nevertheless, he does
understand that mothers have a significant role (though they are not reduced to that role) in the upbringing of their children. Finally, Parsons, I believe, has downplayed the significance of the element of resistance. Surely if
the child is to grow into an individual, he or she must at some point differ-
entiate from the parent and begin to express an identity that, while forged
in and through parental unstinting love, must aim at standing in an equal
power relationship with the initial care-givers. This equality of power need
not, of course, threaten the love that the now grown individuals can con-

tinue to express for each other. Freedom, equality, and friendship, as Macmurray has always insisted, go together in an indissoluble bond. Only a mother with an extraordinary love for her child can take on the role of helping her child through the struggle of resistance.

Without resistance of some kind, which the mother can enable, there would be no need for justice in the family relationship. Justice must be present in any deeply personal relationship precisely because the partners are distinct individuals. As Wong has argued, justice is "relevant in bringing out ways in which family members are to be treated alike in and identifying the morally relevant aspects in which a family can be a group of potential equals."[46] Susan Okin has nicely put the point that a suitably transformed family, one in which the "gendered and inegalitarian structure" has been challenged, can be a place where "all people care for others on a day-to-day basis and, through doing so, . . . learn to reconcile their own ambitions and desires with those of others and . . . see things from the points of view of others who may differ from themselves in important respects."[47] Mother and father are crucial agents in this double work of both transforming the family and of transforming the social structures through political action in order to make them supportive of the family when they threaten to undermine it through practices and institutions that valorize the autonomous, self-sufficient, acquisitive individual who seeks freedom from others rather than freedom for others.

No family is sufficient unto itself as long as it exists within a larger society. This leads naturally to Macmurray's contribution to contemporary thinking on the nation-state and the practices of democracy.

NOTES

1. See Roberto Alejandro, "Rawls's Communitarianism," in *Canadian Journal of Philosophy* 23 (March 1993): 75–100.

2. John Rawls, *A Theory of Justice* (Cambridge, Mass.: Harvard University Press, 1971), 442.

3. Rawls, *A Theory of Justice*, 445.

4. Rawls, *A Theory of Justice*, 525.

5. David B. Wong, "Community, Diversity, and Confucianism," in *In the Company of Others: Perspectives on Community, Family, and Culture*, ed. Nancy B. Snow (Lanham, Md.: Rowman & Littlefield, 1996), 30.

6. Alejandro, "Rawls's Communitarianism," 94.

7. Fairbairn (1943) quoted in James Jones, *Contemporary Psychoanalysis and Religion* (New Haven, Conn.: Yale University Press, 1991), 13.

8. Jay R. Greenberg and Stephen A. Mitchell, *Object Relations in Psychoanalytic Theory* (Cambridge, Mass.: Harvard University Press, 1983), 156.

9. Greenberg and Mitchell, *Object Relations in Psychoanalytic Theory*, 156–57.

10. Greenberg and Mitchell, *Object Relations in Psychoanalytic Theory*, 158.

11. The mother is normally the paradigm of the significant other with whom the child has continuing relationships. The question that Macmurray and object-relations theorists never fully answer however is whether the gender of the parent makes a crucial difference in the child's development of healthy relationality.

12. Greenberg and Mitchell, *Object Relations in Psychoanalytic Theory*, 159.

13. Greenberg and Mitchell, *Object Relations in Psychoanalytic Theory*, 195.

14. Greenberg and Mitchell, *Object Relations in Psychoanalytic Theory*, 160.

15. Nancy Chodrow, "Toward a Relational Individualism: The Mediation of the Self Through Psychoanalysis," in *Reconstructing Individualism: Autonomy, Individuality, and the Self in Western Thought*, ed. Thomas C. Heller, Morton Sosna, and David E. Wellbery (Stanford, Calif.: Stanford University Press, 1986), 201.

16. Chodrow, "Toward a Relational Individualism," 204.

17. Harry Guntrip, quoted in Greenberg and Mitchell, *Object Relations in Psychoanalytic Theory*, 219.

18. Carol Gilligan, "Remapping the Moral Domain: New Images of the Self in Relationship," in Heller, Sosna, and Wellbery, *Reconstructing Individualism*, 238.

19. Gilligan, "Remapping the Moral Domain," 242.

20. Gilligan, "Remapping the Moral Domain," 249.

21. Gilligan, "Remapping the Moral Domain," 250.

22. Susan Moller Okin, *Justice, Gender, and the Family* (New York: Basic Books, 1989), 22.

23. Okin, *Justice, Gender, and the Family*, 72.

24. Jean Bethke Elshtain, *Public Man, Private Woman: Women in Social and Political Thought* (Princeton, N.J.: Princeton University Press, 1981), 322.

25. Elshtain, *Public Man, Private Woman*, 323.

26. Elshtain, *Public Man, Private Woman*, 328.

27. Elshtain, *Public Man, Private Woman*, 332–33.

28. Elshtain, *Public Man, Private Woman*, 337.

29. Elshtain, *Public Man, Private Woman*, 344–45.

30. David B. Wong, "On Flourishing and Finding One's Identity in Community," in *Midwest Studies in Philosophy*, vol. 13, *Ethical Theory: Character and Virtue*, ed. Peter A. French, Theodore E. Uehling Jr., and Howard K. Wettstein (Notre Dame, Ind.: University of Notre Dame Press, 1988), 333.

31. Laurance Thomas, "Moral Motivation: Kantians Vs. Humeans," in *Midwest Studies in Philosophy*, 380.

32. Robert Adams, "Common Projects and Moral Virtue," in *Midwest Studies in Philosophy*, 305.

33. Laurence Thomas, *Living Morally* (Philadelphia: Temple University Press, 1989), viii.

34. Thomas, *Living Morally*, 29.

35. Thomas, *Living Morally*, 60.

36. Thomas, *Living Morally*, 82.

37. Thomas, *Living Morally*, 88.

38. John Macmurray, *Reason and Emotion* (New York: Barnes and Noble, 1962), 109.

39. Macmurray, *Reason and Emotion*, 111.

40. John Macmurray, "Conditions of Marriage Today," in *Marriage Guidance*, 9.12, 1965, ed. Charles F. Davey, 385. It is in David Fergusson, "Macmurray's Philosophy of the Family," *Appraisal* 1 (October 1996): 73.

41. Macmurray, *Reason and Emotion*, 114.

42. Macmurray, *Reason and Emotion*, 138.

43. John Costello, *John Macmurray: A Biography* (Edinburgh: Floris Books, 2002), 127.

44. Susan Parsons, "The Relevance of Macmurray for a Feminist Theology of Action," in *John Macmurray: Critical Perspectives*, ed. David Fergusson and Nigel Dower (New York: Peter Lang, 2002), 148. The Macmurray quote is from *Persons in Relation* (New York: Harper and Brothers, 1961); reprinted, with an introduction by Frank G. Kirkpatrick (London: Humanities Press International, 1991), 89.

45. Parsons, "The Relevance of Macmurray for a Feminist Theology of Action," 149–50.

46. Wong, "On Care and Justice Within the Family," 23.

47. Okin, *Justice, Gender, and the Family*, 119.

10

DEMOCRACY, HUMAN NATURE, AND THE NATION-STATE

Unlike many political philosophies today, John Macmurray's has a strong normative dimension. This normative element is intimately tied to his ontology of the human person as created for fulfillment in and through fellowship, mutuality, and love. Thus he is not content simply to *describe* the nature of social relations while refraining from a moral evaluation of whether they approximate or deviate from the ideal of human fulfillment. Unlike John Rawls, who avoids a metaphysical foundation for political philosophy, Macmurray believes that human nature develops more fully under some ontological/political conditions than others. The ultimate form of its fulfillment, of course, is in and through what he calls community. Without the valorization of community, he would have no way of articulating what he believes to be the proper relationship between community and society.

The relation between community and society always remains complex, ambiguous, and, up to a point, conflictual. Given Macmurray's strong and repeated emphasis on the resistance between persons that is necessary if they are to grow into authentic individuals with distinct identities living in a state of interdependence (neither isolating independence nor slavish dependence), relations of an indirect, impersonal kind (the heart of a society) will always be necessary. And given the tendency of communities, in practice if not in intention, to become self-enclosed and exclusionary, the counter-weight of societies will always be necessary for the successful functioning of communities. The politics practiced in society can invigorate the power of resisting the subordination of the individual to groupthink within the community. The experience of deeper, more fulfilling relations within the community can provide the politics of a society with an ideal toward which to direct its efforts. Communities, which by their nature are supportive, heterocentric, and focused on developing the full potential of unique individuals, can become ideal supportive "sites of resistance" through which persons can learn the techniques of differentiating themselves from others, expressing themselves as themselves, and finding voices that both reflect their individual interests and are empowered to participate in a common conversation. Without these nurturing sites of resistance, individuals would be less well-prepared for the impersonal deployment of power in a social world focused on justice rather than love.

At some point, however, for the relation between society and community to be at its healthiest, a judgment about human nature and human persons in relation must be made. Jean Bethke Elshtain has correctly observed that theories of human nature cannot be excised from political thought. "Without the articulation of what persons are, or can become, a theory of politics remains, at best, incomplete."[1] In addition, she argues, a complete account of human beings in social relation must include "a vision of the complex human subject, a coherent account of the nature of the relations between individuals and society, and an assessment of those moral determinations any responsible theory of historic agency requires."[2] It would be hard to find a statement more clearly expressing the need for what John Macmurray's political philosophy tried to provide.

Political philosopher William Sullivan has noted that in any political philosophy "what is ultimately at issue is the radical question of what is a worthwhile life."[3] John Macmurray devoted his entire philosophical career to addressing this issue. He insisted, contrary to the themes of much contemporary deconstructionist postmodernism, that human nature, at its core, was pretty much the same across historical times and cultures. He knew that it differed in its cultural modes and individual expressions. But underneath the glorious flowering of human nature in a multiplicity of cultural and individual forms, it still found its greatest and most satisfying expression and fulfillment in love, mutuality, trust, and fellowship.

To the extent that much contemporary political philosophy is built on the assumption that human nature is essentially self-centered, ego-driven, aggressive, and competitive, Macmurray's philosophy of the person will find little resonance. But other voices in the philosophical and scientific fields are beginning to question this negative view of human nature. As Andrew Levine has pointed out, today's pessimism (or what is often called its "realism") about human nature "rests on considerations that are no more substantiated, philosophically or empirically," than those to which he appeals in defense of his own self-described "utopian scheme."[4] We have already touched on the work of the object-relations theorists as providing a psychological basis for understanding human nature as essentially relational and loving. An important new empirical study by natural and social scientists provides an initially very promising confirmation of the conviction that empathy and altruism based on a sense of a common humanity are deeper and more explanatory of human behavior than egotism and rational choice theory. Kristen Monroe, in the field of political psychology, has summarized many of these empirical findings when she says that the belief that self-interest is the driving force of our political theories "fail[s] to detect much that is central in other aspects of political and social life. It will be a major advance for social science to construct new theories that embrace a richer conceptualization of the self"[5] that is actually truer to the reality of altruism and love embedded deep in the human psyche and genes.

Even from more politically "realist" thinkers there is a growing recognition of the relational/loving nature of human persons that must be dealt with by any adequate political philosophy. Branko Horvat, a contemporary socialist, has argued, drawing on the early Marx and on Polish philosopher Marek Fritzhand, that human nature needs belongingness and love. Fritzhand says that "Man can only achieve real happiness and perfection when he associates his own happiness and perfection with those of others."[6] Horvat goes on to affirm that "the morality of human beings in this new [socialist] society will not be alienated morality which makes an *obligation* of mutual love, treats love as *self-sacrifice*, as contrary to real interests of individuals. According to this new morality, love is a natural phenomenon of human life, it is *self-affirmation* of man in his relation with other people."[7]

Stephen Elkin, continuing this theme, has said that "the central political problem might be phrased as the creation and maintenance of desirable forms of relation we might have with one another wherever we are going."[8] Charles W. Anderson, in agreement, says that we need "an idea of a *telos*" if we are to "develop a theory of political deliberation that is appropriate to the political economy of the good society."[9] Macmurray's ontology of the person in relation in community provides both a normative understanding of the "desirable forms of relations" and a "telos" toward which he thinks the politics of society must be aimed if these forms of relation are to be empowered.

As we have seen, Macmurray takes his place alongside those political philosophers such as Benhabib who are advocating the inclusion of a multiplicity of voices engaged in a fully democratic debate over the nature and formation of social policies. Different voices engaged in a common conversation bring out the elements of the unique contributions of distinct persons while at the same time reigning in the centrifugal tendencies present in many liberal democratic societies to produce "factions" aiming only at the satisfaction of their own interests. Politics must be more than a contestation of and for power among disparate and fundamentally hostile groups (or at least groups indifferent to the fate of others unless it impinges on their own). While resistance and difference must be part of any healthy conversation (without them it becomes coercive monologue), the participants must glimpse the possibility of commonalities, of life together, if the conversation is to have any point at all.

(It should be noted in passing that if a multiplicity of voices is truly encouraged, the religious voice cannot be excluded. By religious voice, I don't mean the voice of an institutional interest group but the voice that is shaped by a belief in the deepest possible ontological ground for understanding human persons: what have been understood in the theistic religions as the intentions and acts of God. This is clearly an influence on Macmurray, and while he avoids the institutional/denominational/sectarian implications of that influence, his own vision of persons in relation is profoundly influenced by his conviction that community is God's will for God's human creation. While a society might need only an "overlapping consensus" about the foundations of its vision of community, part of that consensus needs to be drawn from the voices of those who articulate a religious understanding of its sources of the self.)

Macmurray would also, I think, join with those who advocate a robust conception of democratic polity that balances equal participation of all with a strong sense of a common good for all. Macmurray was unstinting in his affirmation of the freedom of individuals. But this was not the negative freedom simply to be left alone by others.[10] It was, rather, the freedom that strong democracies enhance: the freedom to become oneself in and through relations with others. Freedom from others is a dead-end because it cuts off the sources of the self that ultimately empower and nurture it. True freedom is the ability to act, with the least amount of hindrance, upon those intentions that will lead to the fulfillment of one's self. In a social setting, freedom would require both supportive mechanisms (e.g., adequate health care, economic resources, educational opportunities, fellowship, etc.) and limitations on obstacles to the development of the self (e.g., reducing as much as possible the hostile and inhibiting conditions of racial and gender discrimination). The exact determination of these mechanisms would be left to what Macmurray calls the participatory, democratic "devices of politics" subordinated to an overarching vision of what persons can become in just and humane societies as well as in loving and compassionate communities. A truly free person is one who acts without arbitrary constraint and with an aim toward being himself, being real. Macmurray has argued that freedom, in the end, is doing what it is one's nature to do: "when ever a thing does of itself what it is its own nature to do, we say that it acts freely. . . . To be free, then, is to express one's nature in action. . . . The free action flows from our own nature."[11] As we have seen, for Macmurray this means that true freedom can only occur in community or fellowship. It occurs not in the absence of others but rather in their presence as supportive and loving partners in relationship who have subordinated fear to love.

Philip Pettit has suggested a similar notion of freedom as nondomination in the presence of other people, "not the absence of domination gained by isolation. . . . It is a social ideal whose realization presupposes the presence of a number of mutually interactive agents."[12] The more one can eliminate the possibility of other people arbitrarily interfering in one's life-in-loving-relation, the less one will fear others and the more trust between them will develop. As Pettit argues, in a way that I think would secure Macmurray's consent, "a decent legal and political order is only possible in a society where there is a lot of active, successful . . . trusting and a relatively intense level of civil life . . . associated with the making of relationships, and the pursuing of common ends, beyond the motivating confines of the family but not yet under the auspices of a coercive state. . . . Unless people are willing to accept various forms of reliance and to trust themselves personally to one another . . . they shall not be able to enjoy the best that is available in the way of non-domination."[13]

The pursuit of common ends, to which Pettit refers, echoes a theme that at one time had resonance in American political philosophy. As historians Gordon Wood, Alan Heimert, and others have argued, the concept of the common or public good as having a moral priority over the private or individual good was advanced by political and religious leaders at the end of the eighteenth century when the founders of the new nation were deciding what form of government it should adopt.

Wood argues that "the sacrifice of individual interests to the greater good of the whole formed the essence of republicanism and comprehended for Americans the idealistic goal of their Revolution."[14] It was assumed by numerous religious and political leaders that the interests of the society and those of its individual members were one. Alan Heimert recalls the words of one evangelical preacher, Nathaniel Niles, who could serenely assume that genuine freedom came not from exercising individual liberty but from life in community. "'A free spirit,' he insisted, 'a spirit that seeks the highest good of the community' was the only being who would 'experience all the pleasures of liberty.'"[15] Niles was particularly critical of what was eventually to become the basic principle of liberal political philosophy: that government exists to protect private interests. Referring to Locke's *Second Treatise of Government*, Niles charged that the social contract described there was a fiction because "'there were no private interests antecedent to compact, but such as had been taken by usurpation.' The notion of government as an instrument for mutual defense of individual property 'is the maxim on which pirates and gangs of robbers live in a kind of unity.'"[16]

The notion of the individual free from all constraining ties to others was regarded by most clergy in the eighteenth century as equivalent to the sin of selfishness. The negatively free individual was considered rootless, immature, and disconnected from the bonds that alone could make him or her whole.[17] On the basis of this understanding of the self in community, Barry Shain has concluded that much of today's political philosophy "has falsely reified individualism into America's chosen political ideology [and] as a consequence, a long and rich tradition of American political thought has been ignored. What has been largely overlooked is a normative theory of the good political life that is enduring, democratic, and communal."[18]

Of course, as any student of American history knows, this democratic communal ideal was ultimately replaced by the factionalism that James Madison cleverly exploited into a philosophy of limited government. Madison believed that self-interest could never be subordinated successfully to ideals of the common good. The parts of the whole would always be, to some degree, in opposition to each other. The Madisonian genius was to play the conflicting parts to a draw. The society itself, he said, "will be broken into so many parts, interests, and classes of citizens, that the rights of individuals, or of the minority, will be in little danger from interested combinations of the majority."[19] Wood calls Madison's political vision a "kinetic theory of politics, such a crumbling of political and social interests, such an atomization of authority, such a parceling of power." And "once the people were thought to be composed of various interests in opposition to one another . . . the people were [no longer seen as] an order organically tied together by their unity of interest but rather an agglomeration of hostile individuals coming together for mutual benefit to construct a society."[20] In such a political climate, the ideals that Macmurray has articulated seem to find little fertile ground in which to grow. Wood, perhaps surprisingly, is not overly pessimistic about the possibility of reviving a sense of society that seeks to embody some of these ideals. He has said that the discovery of an idealistic strain in American political thought at the end of the eighteenth century, a strain that was "*not* always liberal (in the sense of favoring equal personal rights) or capitalistic or individualistic" may convince some people that "maybe we're not destined to remain what we had become."[21] While there is clearly a danger that these community ideals will devolve into the worst forms of communitarianism (which run the risk of a totalitarian organicism in which individuals becomes merely factors functioning to serve the whole and thereby losing their own freedom), the notion of society standing in creative tension with community, as outlined by Macmurray's political philosophy, could be revived as a strong metaphysical/political base for an inclusionary democratic republic.

In this gap between the ideals of individual-affirming community and the present reality of rampant conflictual individualism,[22] politics could become the vehicle of social transformation. There is no reason it should be reduced simply to the contest for power between interest groups. There are many issues that could become the occasion for transformation of the American consciousness about community. One example, among many, is the moral challenge of providing decent health care for all Americans. As we struggle to figure out how to balance the costs of such provision with the fairness toward those who would pay these costs, it would be inevitable that citizens will raise questions about their bonds to others. Illness, perhaps more than anything else, reveals the vulnerability and common humanity of the (temporarily) well and sick. Within families, illness requires extraordinary sacrifices by some members for the sake of others. A politics that moves beyond the family to the citizenry as a whole could carry the insights and values of caring and compassion into the larger economic and politic arenas. If as a nation we genuinely tried to extend to all citizens the same level of health care we would expect for our family members, new ways of thinking about ourselves as an extended family, or at least as a society that holds health care to be a common and public good, might emerge. There is no reason access to quality health care should not be regarded as being as important as access to quality education for all children. But only a conviction that we share a common humanity and are closely bound to each other in a common life can bring this importance to life in a politically meaningful way.

There are those today who would argue that the ideals of community and a society built on the notion of a common good that Macmurray espouses would be best handled in an individualistic market-based society by the work of philanthropy or charity. Charity is, after all, love in action, and religious sources, especially from the Jewish and Christian traditions, have deeply influenced the work of charity. It would seem, therefore, that Macmurray would find the work of charity to be a major part of his notion of a good society. I think this assumption is wrong, at least in one major respect.

It is generally accepted that liberal market-based societies have three sectors: the business or for-profit sector, the government sector, and the charitable or philanthropic sector. The business sector creates the wealth that the society requires to meet its basic human needs; the government sector collects a portion of that wealth and determines, by public legislation, the uses to which it will be put to meet the basic needs of its citizens; and the philanthropic sector both fills in the gaps in the provision of public services and provides creative thinking and experimentation about how society's needs can be met more effectively. There is no doubt that the philanthropic spirit is essential both to nurturing the habits of the heart that make a society humane and to meeting those human needs that for the time being are unmet. Philanthropy also reminds us that love toward others is not simply reducible to legally enforced and coercive forms of justice.

However, there is much about philanthropy that fails to fully meet the systematic extension of justice to all persons in a society. Individual acts of charity cannot solve the systemic causes that produce poverty, illness, poor education, and racism, for example. Institutional forms of philanthropy are, in addition, undemocratic in that their policies are not determined by the vote of those they are seeking to help. The wealthy and powerful who constitute the boards of philanthropic foundations decide, without citizen input, what problems to address and what programs to support. Philanthropy also tends to disguise and divert attention from the unjust power relations between the rich and the poor in society. Charity depends on the good heart of the giver, not on the rights of the recipient: it assumes no universal social or legal *obligation* to help the economically disadvantaged. As a result charity, both individual and institutional, is often arbitrary and selective. It rarely challenges the principles and systems of business and law that provide the philanthropists the power and freedom to secure the money they use to dispense their charity.

One criticism often leveled at philanthropic foundations is that they represent "relatively unregulated and unaccountable concentrations of power and wealth which buy talent, promote causes, and establish an agenda of what merits society's attention, delaying and preventing more radical, structural change."[23] Charity alone simply cannot address the complex societal problem, for example, of extending quality health care to all persons. No amount of individual or foundational philanthropy can build and sustain all the hospitals, train and retain the doctors and nurses, invest in the best of medical technology, and pay for the services those unable to pay out of pocket will need. The medical infrastructure is so vast and complex, only a society-wide system can support it. And only through a democratically controlled system of taxation developing and maintaining this infrastructure can equity for all citizens throughout the country be ensured. To expect love alone to handle these issues of a complex democracy is to fall into what Macmurray called the mistake of a minor mutuality. "Without justice," he argued, "morality becomes illusory and sentimental, the mere appearance of morality: . . . justice safeguards the inclusiveness of the moral reference, and so the unity of the Other. To be generous without being just is to be generous to some at the expense of others; and so to produce a minor mutuality which is hostile to the interests of the larger community [society]."[24]

A genuine democracy that takes justice seriously would rely less on philanthropy and more on democratically determined limits on business and government to provide basic services meeting basic human rights. As Allen Buchanan has suggested: "that the needy no longer have to rely exclusively upon the uncoordinated, highly inefficient, and arbitrarily selective charitable acts of individuals, that being recognized as a subject of justice is not thought to depend upon one's relative power but upon one's fundamental status as a human being, that the humanity of all who are human is acknowledged, that society is beginning to take responsibility for designing institutions so as to include more individuals as full participants in social life, and that the international community is slowing working toward guaranteeing all individuals access to a political order that will protect their basic rights—these are the major steps toward collective moral improvement,"[25] steps that I am convinced Macmurray would fully endorse.

BEYOND THE NATION-STATE

Buchanan's comment alludes to the international community. Macmurray's work also points toward a notion of a global society, but not in any naive way. In a 1956 article, "Towards World Unity,"[26] Macmurray urges a world government. He believes that *in practice* if not yet in theory, the world "behaves inevitably as a single society."[27] The *fact* of world unity is seen most clearly in the economic interdependencies among the nations of the world. Macmurray is acutely conscious that the autonomy of sovereign states belies the practical dependence of struggling new nations on the older, industrialized, and wealthier nations. The only way for this mutual interdependence to be reflected effectively is through a political arrangement that brings a legal system to all the nations of the world, in short, a world government.[28] This is the only way to attain true global justice. Personal or individual efforts to bring equity to international bodies will not suffice. "The only way in which justice or some approximation to justice can be achieved in the interdependence of our human activities is through some impersonal system which performs the adjustment of itself." At the international level this means "some kind of world justice."[29]

Macmurray insists that this is "realistic political thinking." This means finding "the kind of society that is possible; and its possibility is made by the circumstances, by the objective facts of the situation."[30] We need, he argues, world unity without dictatorship based on force and the suppression of freedom.[31] The only realistic possibility must be grounded in a "common humanity." And that is precisely what he has attempted to provide in his metaphysical treatment of the nature of persons in relation. He assumes, of course, that this treatment is consistent with a Hebraic-Christian understanding of reality and so concludes his treatise on world unity by asserting that "the social teaching of Christianity has become the only practical politics."[32]

This view is not entirely at odds with the stark judgment of John Dunn that "nationalism is the starkest political shame of the twentieth century." Dunn's indictment is based on his belief that nationalism is nothing more than "a habit of accommodation of which we feel the moral shabbiness readily enough ourselves" because it violates "the universalist heritage of a natural law conceived either in terms of Christianity or of secular rationalism."[33] The universalist thrust of Macmurray's work on community, grounded in his conviction that we are all children of a single God, underlies his interest in something that extends beyond the nation-state. Macmurray even suggests that he does not want a world state based on the model of the nation-state. "I find the dream of a super-state governing the whole world something of a nightmare," he asserts; "the States we know are as they are largely because they are exclusive and have to face outward, armed to the teeth, to defend their exclusiveness and sovereign independence."[34] Instead of such a superstate, he urges a "world fellowship" in which the barriers of nationalism could be brought down. Consistent with his tendency to judge the devices of politics by their effectiveness in achieving the aims of community and justice, he argues that we would then be free "to draw such boundaries on the map as were most convenient for the purposes of co-operative activity; and the co-ordination of these units of political organization, in so far as that was necessary, and for this special purpose or that, could be arranged without difficulty, without the need for a single sovereign centre of power which should be omnicompetent."[35]

In his approach to global justice, Macmurray reveals the continuing elements of his political thought. There is a vision of a world fellowship that points beyond the nation-state as a collective form of self-interest; there is a reference to a common or shared humanity that transcends cultural and parochial boundaries; there is a pragmatism (despite his dislike of the term) about how to begin to implement the vision of a global fellowship; and there is his continuing distrust of a politically coercive power that stands over the individual-in-community, limiting his or her freedom and growth. Macmurray died, of course, before this vision could make much headway.

MACMURRAY AND TONY BLAIR

Ironically, Macmurray's most well-known contribution to the politics of the present has come through the influence he is alleged to have had on one of Europe's most important political figures, British Prime Minister Tony Blair, his most recent self-proclaimed political disciple. Blair has said that "if you really want to understand what I'm all about, you have to take a look at a guy called John Macmurray. It's all there."[36] Blair encountered the works of Macmurray while studying at Oxford.

Because of Blair's avowed indebtedness to Macmurray, the British press scurried to find out more about this moral and religious philosopher. While many commentators revealed that they had not really read Macmurray (some calling him a Marxist, some a communitarian, some saying he completely neglected politics), there was at least a resurgence of interest in his thought. Blair has said that Macmurray had helped him to see "the coincidence between the philosophical theory of Christianity and left-of-centre politics."[37] Whatever the exact linkage between Macmurray's thought and Blair's politics, it is clear that the concept of community is at its center. What is not nearly as clear is the use to which Blair puts the concept of community in his political practice. At one level it is faithful to Macmurray's notion that the isolated individual is not capable of being a full and complete human being as long as he or she lacks strong relationships with others. At another level, community has become in Blair's so-called "Third Way" or "New Labour" politics a catch-all phrase for, as he put it in 1999, "a concept of a modern civic society that is founded on opportunity and responsibility, rights and duties going together."[38]

Leftist critics of Blair argue that this understanding of community is really an attempt to move away from society's obligation to the individual and toward a much stronger notion of the individual's responsibilities to the society. Nevertheless, the official language of the new Labour Party affirms that it is a "democratic socialist party" that believes that "by the strength of our common endeavour we achieve more than we achieve alone, so as to create for each of us the means to realize our true potential and for all of us a community in which power, wealth and opportunity are in the hands of the many not the few; where the rights we enjoy reflect the duties we owe and where we live together freely in a spirit of solidarity, tolerance and respect."[39]

Blair is obviously employing the word "community" where Macmurray would have used the word "society." There is little in Blair's use of the term "community" of the mutuality, heterocentrism, and love that Macmurray felt were essential to life in community. Blair also seems comfortable reconciling a free market with his view of a democratic socialist society. Macmurray seemed far more uncomfortable with this relationship. But nearly a half-century separated Macmurray's analysis of the political and economic life of Great Britain from Blair's politics at the turn of the twenty-first century. Blair has said that the Third Way "stands for a modernized social democracy, passionate in its commitment to social justice and the goals of the centre-left, but flexible, innovative and forward-looking in the means to achieve them. It is founded on the values [of] democracy, liberty, justice, mutual obligation and internationalism."[40] While obviously avoiding the dangers of rigid, doctrinaire ideology (which Macmurray would also have shunned), Blair's statement is so open-ended as to make it impossible to determine if his actual policies are consistent with or faithful to Macmurray's political understanding. How flexible is it? How do individual liberty and a commitment to social justice co-exist in practice? Is it pragmatic in a way Macmurray would have accepted as realistic to the task at hand?

One of the persistent criticisms of Blair is that his articulation of the Third Way is so rhetorical, inclusive, and ambiguous that it can justify almost any politics. In this respect the jury is still out on whether he is carrying forward a Macmurrian political philosophy. Nevertheless, it is significant that one of the major politicians of the early twenty-first century is a man who has explicitly claimed the decisive influence of John Macmurray.

CONCLUSION

The promise and potential of Macmurray's political thought have yet to be fully appreciated in the world of political philosophy. Apart from his ambiguous influence on Tony Blair, there are few politically active persons who are guided by his ideas. He falls uneasily between those who think primarily of politics through a social science perspective as the work of agents of rational choice and those from the religious sphere who see politics through hazy mists of love and mutuality without attention to the economic and political conditions under which they are enacted in a complex democratic society. Macmurray bridged these two worlds, but today, most practitioners in both worlds would regard his work as not well anchored to mainstream social science data or to theological doctrine.

Nevertheless, I believe that his contribution to political philosophy today lies in the dialectical relation he establishes between community and society, justice and love, built upon a metaphysical foundation of persons-in-relation. Only within a more comprehensive philosophical framework can these crucial dimensions of the human self in relation with others be brought into harmony with each other. Macmurray was able both to ground his understanding of the fulfillment of human persons in a philosophy of the personal and to articulate ways in which that understanding could be given concrete application. Through his philosophy, he brings the possibility of transcending the narrow cultural boundaries that have confined much political and moral philosophy in recent years and giving us the "something more" that is needed if political philosophy and theology are each to contribute to the flourishing of the human being. By his insistence on political equality and justice, centered in his notion of resistance, his work can contribute to the ongoing struggles for economic justice, and the enfranchisement of traditionally marginalized persons and groups, especially women and minorities. He has much to say about the need to preserve individual freedom and the spiritual dimension in societies that insist upon justice. He also reminds those who focus on love and mutuality that these dimensions of human relationship do not occur in a political or economic vacuum. He has also restored normativity to a discipline often devoid of any reference to values. He has brought the insights of religion into the political field without institutionalizing or parochializing them. He has brought the virtue of trust squarely into the heart of political philosophy without reducing it to the sentimental. He has refused to allow the values of community to be reduced to the politics of society. At the same time, he has not valorized love to the point where he has become unmindful of the necessity of empowering love, family, and mutuality with the appropriate economic and social conditions. He has articulated a vision of a world politics that is neither naive nor crassly political. His is a voice that reflected and challenged his own time: because of its grounding in a philosophy of the personal that transcends any particular historical time, it is now a voice that challenges us as well.

NOTES

1. Jean Bethke Elshtain, *Real Politics* (Baltimore: Johns Hopkins University Press, 1997), 14–15.

2. Elshtain, *Real Politics*, 179.

3. William M. Sullivan, *Reconstructing Public Philosophy* (Berkeley: University of California Press, 1982), 10.

4. Andrew Levine, *Rethinking Liberal Equality* (Ithaca, N.Y.: Cornell University Press, 1998), 81.

5. Kristen Renwick Monroe, "Explicating Altruism," in *Altruism and Altruistic Love*, ed. Stephen G. Post, Lynn G. Underwood, Jeffrey P. Schloss, and William B. Hurlbut (Oxford: Oxford University Press, 2002), 114. While the classic sociobiological approach to human nature still stresses the "selfish gene" theory, there are many social scientists such as Monroe who are finding, through their research, that this emphasis is greatly overdone. See also Monroe, *The Heart of Altruism* (Princeton, N.J.: Princeton University Press, 1996).

6. Marek Fritzhand, in Branko Horvat, *The Political Economy of Socialism* (Armonk, N.Y.: M. E. Sharpe, 1982), 101. The quote is from Fritzhand, "Marx's Ideal of Man," in E. Fromm, *Socialist Humanism* (New York: Doubleday, 1966), 172–73.

7. Horvat, *The Political Economy of Socialism*, 101.

8. Stephen Elkin, "Conclusion," in *The Constitution of Good Societies*, ed. Karol Edward Soltan and Stephen L. Elkin (University Park: Pennsylvania State University Press, 1996), 200.

9. Charles W. Anderson, "How to Make a Good Society," in Soltan and Elkin, *The Constitution of Good Societies*, 109.

10. The influence and pervasiveness of this notion of freedom in the United States is well-documented in Robert Bellah et al., *Habits of the Heart* (Berkeley: University of California Press, 1986).

11. Macmurray, *Freedom in the Modern World*, Broadcast Talks on Modern Problems, with a preface by C. A. Siepmann (London: Faber and Faber, 1932), 166.

12. Philip Pettit, *Republicanism: A Theory of Freedom and Government* (Oxford: Clarendon Press, 1997), 66.

13. Pettit, *Republicanism*, 262, 266.

14. Gordon S. Wood, *The Creation of the American Republic 1776–1787* (Chapel Hill: University of North Carolina Press, 1969), 53.

15. Alan Heimert, *Religion and the American Mind* (Cambridge, Mass.: Harvard University Press, 1966), 456.

16. Heimert, *Religion and the American Mind*, 515.

17. Barry Alan Shain, *The Myth of American Individualism* (Princeton, N.J.: Princeton University Press, 1994), 98–100.

18. Shain, *The Myth of American Individualism*, xviii.

19. James Madison, *The Federalist*, no. 51, quoted in Wood, *The Creation of the American Republic*, 605.

20. Wood, *The Creation of the American Republic*, 606–7.

21. Gordon Wood, "Hellfire Politics," review of J. P. Diggins, *The Lost Soul of American Politics*, in *New York Review of Books*, February 1985, 29.

22. See Bellah et al., *Habits of the Heart*, for a careful but precise depiction of the tension between the ideal of community and the practice of individualism in American life today.

23. Robert Arnove, *Philanthropy and Cultural Imperialism* (Boston: G. K. Hall, 1980), quoted in J. Craig Jenkins, "Social Movement Philanthropy and American Democracy," in *Philanthropic Giving: Studies in Varieties and Goals*, ed. Richard Magat (New York: Oxford University Press, 1989), 292.

24. John Macmurray, *Persons in Relation* (New York: Harper and Brothers, 1961); reprinted, with an introduction by Frank G. Kirkpatrick (London: Humanities Press International, 1991), 189.

25. Allen Buchanan, "Charity, Justice, and Moral Progress," in *Giving: Western Ideas of Philanthropy*, ed. J. B. Schneewind (Bloomington: Indiana University Press, 1996), 114–15.

26. John Macmurray, "Towards World Unity" (Toronto: John Macmurray Society, 1956).

27. Macmurray, "Towards World Unity," 7.

28. Macmurray, "Towards World Unity," 11.

29. Macmurray, "Towards World Unity," 12.

30. Macmurray, "Towards World Unity," 13.

31. Macmurray, "Towards World Unity," 15.

32. Macmurray, "Towards World Unity," 19.

33. John Dunn, *Western Political Theory in the Face of the Future* (Cambridge: Cambridge University Press, 1979), 57–59.

34. Macmurray, *Conditions of Freedom* (London: Faber and Faber, 1950), 105.

35. Macmurray, *Conditions of Freedom*, 105.

36. Quotation found in Leo Abse, *Tony Blair: The Man Behind the Smile* (London: Robson Books, 2001), 99.

37. Abse, *Tony Blair*, 99. Abse is extremely critical of Blair and says of this quote that it is "fiction." He also regards Macmurray as a "minor figure in academic theology" (99).

38. Norman Fairclough, *New Labour, New Language?* (New York: Routledge, 2000), 38.

39. This quotation from Clause Four of the Labour Party's rulebook of 1998 is found in Melanie A. Sully, *The New Politics of Tony Blair* (Boulder, Colo.: Social Science Monographs, distributed by New York: Columbia University Press, 2000), 5.

40. Sully, *The New Politics of Tony Blair*, 85.

BIBLIOGRAPHY

JOHN MACMURRAY: BOOKS

The Boundaries of Science. London: Faber and Faber, 1939.

The Clue to History. London: SCM Press, 1938.

Conditions of Freedom. London: Faber and Faber, 1950.

Constructive Democracy. London: Faber and Faber, 1943.

Creative Society: A Study of the Relation of Christianity to Communism. London: SCM Press, 1935.

Freedom in the Modern World. Broadcast Talks on Modern Problems. With a preface by C. A. Siepmann. London: Faber and Faber, 1932.

Interpreting the Universe. London: Faber and Faber, 1933.

Persons in Relation. New York: Harper and Brothers, 1961. Reprinted, with an introduction by Frank G. Kirkpatrick. London: Humanities Press International, 1991.

The Philosophy of Communism. London: Faber and Faber, 1933.

Reason and Emotion. New York: Barnes and Noble, 1962.

Religion in the Modern World. Montreal: Associated Literature Service, 1938.

Search for Reality in Religion. Swarthmore Lecture, 1965. London: George Allen and Unwin, 1965.

The Self as Agent. London: Faber and Faber, 1957. Reprinted, with an introduction by Stanley M. Harrison. London: Humanities Press International, 1991.

The Structure of Religious Experience. London: Faber and Faber, 1936.

JOHN MACMURRAY: ARTICLES

"The Challenge of Communism." In *Christianity and Communism*, by H. G. Wood and John Macmurray. London: Industrial Christian Fellowship, 1934.

"Christianity and Communism: Towards a Synthesis." In *Christianity and the Social Revolution*, edited by John Lewis. London: Victor Gollancz, 1935.

"Christianity—Pagan or Scientific?" *Hibbert Journal* 24 (1925–1926).

"The Coming Election." *British Weekly*, October 24, 1931.

"The Conception of Society." *Proceedings of the Aristotelian Society* 31 (1930–1931).

"Dialectical Materialism as a Philosophy." In *Aspects of Dialectical Materialism*, edited by H. Levy. London: Watts, 1935.

"The Dualism of Mind and Matter." *Philosophy* 10 (1935).

"The Early Development of Marx's Thought." In *Christianity and the Social Revolution*, edited by John Lewis. London: Victor Gollancz, 1935.

"Economic Laws and Social Progress." *Auxiliary Movement* 29 (February 1927).

"Equality." *New Britain*, June 21, 1933.

"Fascism?" *New Britain*, June 7, 1933.

"Freedom in the Personal Nexus." In *Freedom: Its Meaning*, edited by Ruth Nanda Anshen. New York: Harcourt Brace, 1940.

"The Function of Experiment in Knowledge," *Proceedings of the Aristotelian Society* 27 (1926–1927).

"General Smuts as Philosopher." *British Weekly*, January 20, 1927.

"Government by the People." *Journal of Philosophical Studies* 2 (1927).

"Has Religion a Message for To-Day?" *Reynolds's Illustrated News*, November 24, 1935.

"Introductory." In *Some Makers of the Modern Spirit*, edited by John Macmurray. London: Methuen, 1933.

"The Limits of Interference Between Sovereign States," *British Weekly*, December 26, 1929.

"The Modern Spirit: An Essay." In *Some Makers of the Modern Spirit*, edited by John Macmurray. London: Methuen, 1933.

"The Nature and Function of Ideologies." In *Marxism*, edited by J. Middleton Murry. London: Chapman and Hall, 1935.

"The Nature of Philosophy." In *Marxism*, edited by J. Middleton Murry. London: Chapman and Hall, 1935.

"The Nature of Religion." Report of the St. Asaph Conference, August 1938.

"The New Materialism." In *Marxism*, edited by J. Middleton Murry. London: Chapman and Hall, 1935.

"Personality, Freedom and Authority." BBC Broadcast, October 16, 1934.

"The Principle of Personality in Experience." *Proceedings of the Aristotelian Society* 29 (1928–1929).

"The Provisional Basis of the Christian Left." *Christian Left*, February 1938.

"Religion in Russia." Anglo-Soviet Public Relations Association, Leaflet 1, 1942.

"The Religious Task of the Christian Left." *Christian Left*, March 20, 1937.

"Russia and Finland." *Christian Left*, March 1940.

"Socialism and Democracy." *Christian Left*, March 1940.

"Summary." In *Some Makers of the Modern Spirit*, edited by John Macmurray. London: Methuen, 1933.

"Towards World Unity." Toronto: John Macmurray Society, 1956.

"The Unity of Modern Problems." *Journal of Philosophical Studies* 4 (1929).

"Valuations in Fascist and Community States." In *Class Conflict and Social Stratification*, edited by T. H. Marshall. London: LePlay House Press, 1938.

"What About Communism?" *New Britain*, June 14, 1933.

[with others] "The New Magazine, October, 1937," "Christian Left Documents," "The Christian Left: Draft Basis," "Cross, Hammer and Sickle," "The Summer Conference." *Christian Left*, July 15, 1937.

BOOKS BY OTHER AUTHORS

Abse, Leo. *Tony Blair: The Man Behind the Smile.* London: Robson Books, 2001.

Acland, Richard. *Nothing Left to Believe?* London: Longmans Green, 1949.

Acland, Richard. *Questions and Answers from Common Wealth Meetings.* London, 1943.

Ashley, M. P., and C. T. Saunders. *Red Oxford: A History of the Growth of Socialism in the University of Oxford.* Oxford: Oxford University Labour Club, 1930.

Avineri, Shlomo, and Avner De-Shalit, eds. *Communitarianism and Individualism.* New York: Oxford University Press, 1992.

Bellah, Robert, et al. *Habits of the Heart.* Berkeley: University of California Press, 1986.

Benhabib, Seyla. *Situating the Self.* New York: Routledge, 1992.

Calder, Angus. *The People's War.* New York: Pantheon and Random House, 1969.

Cole, G. D. H. *A History of the Labour Party from 1914.* London: Routledge and Kegan Paul, 1948.

Cole, G. D. H. *What Marx Really Meant.* London: Victor Gollancz, 1934.

Costello, John. *John Macmurray: A Biography.* Edinburgh: Floris Books, 2002.

Dunn, John. *Western Political Theory in the Face of the Future.* Cambridge: Cambridge University Press, 1979.

Elshtain, Jean Bethke. *Public Man, Private Woman: Women in Social and Political Thought.* Princeton, NJ: Princeton University Press, 1981.

Elshtain, Jean Bethke. *Real Politics.* Baltimore: Johns Hopkins University Press, 1997.

Fairclough, Norman. *New Labour, New Language?* London: Routledge, 2000.

Fergusson, David, and Nigel Dower, eds. *John Macmurray: Critical Perspectives.* New York: Peter Lang, 2002.

Findlay, J. N. *Hegel: A Re-Examination.* New York: Collier Books, 1962.

French, Peter A., Theodore E. Uehling Jr., and Howard K. Wettstein, eds. *Midwest Studies in Philosophy.* Vol. 13, *Ethical Theory: Character and Virtue.* Notre Dame, Ind.: University of Notre Dame Press, 1988.

Gould, Carol. *Rethinking Democracy: Freedom and Social Cooperation in Politics, Economy, and Society.* Cambridge: Cambridge University Press, 1988.

Gray, J. Glenn, ed. *G. W. F. Hegel: On Art, Religion, Philosophy*. New York: Harper Torchbook, 1970.

Greenberg, Jay R., and Stephen A. Mitchell. *Object Relations in Psychoanalytic Theory*. Cambridge, Mass.: Harvard University Press, 1983.

Hegel, G. W. F. *Hegel's Philosophy of Right*, translated with notes by T. M. Knox. New York: Oxford University Press, 1967.

Hegel, G. W. F. *On Art, Religion, Philosophy*, edited by J. Glenn Gray. New York: Harper and Row, 1970.

Heimert, Alan. *Religion and the American Mind*. Cambridge, Mass.: Harvard University Press, 1966.

Hook, Sidney. *From Hegel to Marx*. Ann Arbor: University of Michigan Press, c. 1950.

Horvat, Branko. *The Political Economy of Socialism*. Armonk, N.Y.: M. E. Sharpe, 1982.

Jackson, T. A. *Dialectics: The Logic of Marxism and Its Critics*. London: Lawrence and Wishart, 1936.

Johann, Robert. *The Pragmatic Meaning of God*. Milwaukee, Wis.: Marquette University Press, 1966.

James, Jones. *Contemporary Psychoanalysis and Religion*. New Haven, Conn.: Yale University Press, 1991.

Kamenka, Eugene. *The Ethical Foundations of Marxism*. New York: Frederick A. Praeger, 1962.

Kirkpatrick, Frank G. *Community: A Trinity of Models*. Washington, D.C.: Georgetown University Press, 1986.

Kirkpatrick, Frank G. *Together Bound: God, History, and the Religious Community*. New York: Oxford University Press, 1994.

Kymlicka, Will. *Contemporary Political Philosophy*. 2nd ed. Oxford: Oxford University Press, 2002.

Levine, Andrew. *Rethinking Liberal Equality*. Ithaca, N.Y.: Cornell University Press, 1998.

Levy, H., et al. *Aspects of Dialectical Materialism*. London: Watts, 1935.

Lewis, John, ed. *Christianity and the Social Revolution*. London: Victor Gollancz, 1935.

Lindsay, A. D. *Karl Marx's Capital: An Introductory Essay*. London: Oxford University Press, 1925.

MacIntyre, Alasdair. *After Virtue*. Notre Dame, Ind.: University of Notre Dame Press, 1981.

Magat, Richard, ed. *Philanthropic Giving: Studies in Varieties and Goals*. New York: Oxford University Press, 1989.

Marx, Karl. *Der Historische Materialismus. Die Fruhschriften*. Herausgegeben von S. Landshut und J. P. Meyer, unter Mitwirkung von F. Salomen. Leipsig: Alfred Kroner Verlag, 1932.

Marx, Karl. *Economic and Philosophic Manuscripts of 1844*, edited with an introduction by Dirk J. Struik, translated by Martin Milligan. New York: International Publishers, 1964.

Marx, Karl. *Grundrisse: Foundations of the Critique of Political Economy* (rough draft), translated by Martin Nicelaus. Harmondsworth, U.K.: Penguin Books, 1973.

Marx, Karl. *The German Ideology*, edited with an introduction by C. J. Arthur. New York: International Publishers, 1970.

McLellan, David, ed. *Karl Marx: Selected Writings*. Oxford: Oxford University Press, 1977.

Meszaros, Istvan. *Marx's Theory of Alienation*. London: Merlin Press, 1970.

Monroe, Kristen Renwick. *The Heart of Altruism*. Princeton, N.J.: Princeton University Press, 1996.

Muller, Jerry Z. *The Mind and the Market*. New York: Alfred A. Knopf, 2002.

Murry, J. Middleton, ed. *Marxism*. London: Chapman and Hall, 1935.

Okin, Susan Moller. *Justice, Gender, and the Family*. New York: Basic Books, 1989.

Ollman, Bertell. *Alienation*. 2nd ed. Cambridge: Cambridge University Press, 1976.

Pettit, Philip. *Republicanism: A Theory of Freedom and Government*. Oxford: Clarendon Press, 1997.

Phillips, Derek L. *Looking Backward: A Critical Appraisal of Communitarian Thought*. Princeton, N.J.: Princeton University Press, 1993.

Post, Stephen G., Lynn G. Underwood, Jeffrey P. Schloss, and William B. Hurlbut, eds. *Altruism and Altruistic Love*. Oxford: Oxford University Press, 2002.

Rader, Melvin. *Marx's Interpretation of History*. New York: Oxford University Press, 1979.

Rawls, John. *A Theory of Justice*. Cambridge, Mass.: Harvard University Press, 1971.

Rossiter, Clinton. *Marxism: The View From America*. New York: Harcourt Brace, 1960.

Schneewind, J. B., ed. *Giving: Western Ideas of Philanthropy*. Bloomington: Indiana University Press, 1996.

Shain, Barry Alan. *The Myth of American Individualism*. Princeton, N.J.: Princeton University Press, 1994.

Soltan, Karol Edward, and Stephen L. Elkin, eds. *The Constitution of Good Societies*. University Park: Pennsylvania State University Press, 1996.

Sullivan, William M. *Reconstructing Public Philosophy*. Berkeley: University of California Press, 1982.

Sully, Melanie A. *The New Politics of Tony Blair*. Boulder, Colo.: Social Science Monographs; distributed by New York: Columbia University Press, 2000.

Laurence Thomas, *Living Morally*. Philadelphia: Temple University Press, 1989.

Wood, Allen W. *Karl Marx*. London: Routledge and Kegan Paul, 1981.

Wood, Gordon S. *The Creation of the American Republic 1776–1787*. Chapel Hill: University of North Carolina Press, 1969.

ARTICLES BY OTHER AUTHORS

Robert Adams. "Common Projects and Moral Virtue." In *Midwest Studies in Philosophy*. Vol. 13, *Ethical Theory: Character and Virtue*, edited by Peter A. French,

Theodore E. Uehling Jr., and Howard K. Wettstein. Notre Dame, Ind.: University of Notre Dame Press, 1988.

Alejandro, Roberto. "Rawls's Communitarianism." *Canadian Journal of Philosophy* 23 (March 1993).

Anderson, Charles W. "How to Make a Good Society." In *The Constitution of Good Societies*, edited by Karol Edward Soltan and Stephen L. Elkin. University Park: Pennsylvania State University Press, 1996.

Buchanan, Allen. "Charity, Justice, and Moral Progress." In *Giving: Western Ideas of Philanthropy*, edited by J. B. Schneewind. Bloomington: Indiana University Press, 1996.

Chodrow, Nancy. "Toward a Relational Individualism: The Mediation of the Self Through Psychoanalysis." In *Reconstructing Individualism: Autonomy, Individuality, and the Self in Western Thought*, edited by Thomas C. Heller, Morton Sosna, and David E. Wellbery. Stanford, Calif.: Stanford University Press, 1986.

Elkin, Stephen. "Conclusion." In *The Constitution of Good Societies*, edited by Karol Edward Soltan and Stephen L. Elkin. University Park: Pennsylvania State University Press, 1996.

Fergusson, David. "Macmurray's Philosophy of the Family." *Appraisal* 1 (October 1996).

Friedman, Marilyn. "Care and Context in Moral Reasoning." In *What Are Friends For? Feminist Perspectives on Personal Relationships and Moral Theory*. Ithaca, N.Y.: Cornell University Press, 1993.

Friedman, Marilyn. "Gendered Morality." In *What Are Friends For? Feminist Perspectives on Personal Relationships and Moral Theory*. Ithaca, N.Y.: Cornell University Press, 1993.

Gilligan, Carol. "Remapping the Moral Domain: New Images of the Self in Relationship." In *Reconstructing Individualism: Autonomy, Individuality, and the Self in Western Thought*, edited by Thomas C. Heller, Morton Sosna, and David E. Wellbery. Stanford, Calif.: Stanford University Press, 1986.

Jenkins, J. Craig. "Social Movement Philanthropy and American Democracy." In *Philanthropic Giving: Studies in Varieties and Goals*, edited by Richard Magat. New York: Oxford University Press, 1989.

Joad, C. E. M. Review of *Marxism*. *Spectator*, March 29, 1935.

Kymlicka, Will. "Liberalism and Communitarianism." *Canadian Journal of Philosophy* 18 (June 1988).

Laird, John. Review of *The Philosophy of Communism*. *Philosophy* 10 (1935).

Lam, Elizabeth. "Does Macmurray Understand Marx?" *Journal of Religion* 20 (1940).

Laski, H. J. Review of *Aspects of Dialectical Materialism*. *New Statesman and Nation*, January 26, 1935.

Lewis, John D. Review of *Marxism*. *American Political Science Review* 29 (1935).

Marx, Karl. "On James Mill." In *Karl Marx: Selected Writings*, edited by David McLellan. Oxford: Oxford University Press, 1977.

Marx, Karl. "Results of the Immediate Process of Production." In *Karl Marx: Selected Writings*, edited by David McLellan. Oxford: Oxford University Press, 1977.

Marx, Karl. "Contribution to the Critique of Hegel's Philosophy of Right." In *On Religion*, by Karl Marx and Friedrich Engels, introduction by Reinhold Niebuhr. New York: Schocken Books, 1964.

Monroe, Kristen Renwick. "Explicating Altruism." In *Altruism and Altruistic Love*, edited by Stephen G. Post, Lynn G. Underwood, Jeffrey P. Schloss, and William B. Hurlbut. Oxford: Oxford University Press, 2002.

Niebuhr, Reinhold. Review of *Christianity and the Social Crisis* and *Creative Society*. *New York Herald Tribune Books*, June 14, 1936.

Niebuhr, Reinhold. Review of *The Clue to History*. *Modern Churchman* 29 (May 1939).

Parsons, Susan. "The Relevance of Macmurray for a Feminist Theology of Action." In *John Macmurray: Critical Perspectives*, edited by David Fergusson and Nigel Dower. New York: Peter Lang, 2002.

Plant, Raymond. "Social Thought." In *The Twentieth Century Mind: History, Ideas, and Literature in Britain*. Vol. 2, *1918–1945*, edited by C. B. Cox and A. E. Dyson. London: Oxford University Press, 1972.

Rawls, John. "The Priority of Rights and Ideas of the Good." *Philosophy and Public Affairs* 17 (1988).

Rawls, John. "Justice as Fairness: Political not Metaphysical." *Philosophy and Public Affairs* 14 (1985).

Sandel, Michael. "The Procedural Republic and the Unencumbered Self." In *Communitarianism and Individualism*, edited by Shlomo Avineri and Avner De-Shalit. New York: Oxford University Press, 1992.

Tawney, R. H. Review of *Christianity and the Social Revolution*. *New Statesman and Nation*, November 9, 1935.

Thomas, Laurance. "Moral Motivation: Kantians vs. Humeans." In *Midwest Studies in Philosophy*. Vol. 13, *Ethical Theory: Character and Virtue*, edited by Peter A. French, Theodore E. Uehling Jr., and Howard K. Wettstein. Notre Dame, Ind.: University of Notre Dame Press, 1988.

Wong, David B. "Community, Diversity, and Confucianism." In *In the Company of Others: Perspectives on Community, Family, and Culture*, edited by Nancy B. Snow. Lanham, Md.: Rowman & Littlefield, 1996.

Wong, David B. "On Flourishing and Finding One's Identity in Community." In *Midwest Studies in Philosophy*. Vol. 13, *Ethical Theory: Character and Virtue*, edited by Peter A. French, Theodore E. Uehling Jr., and Howard K. Wettstein. Notre Dame, Ind.: University of Notre Dame Press, 1988.

Wood, Gordon. "Hellfire Politics." Review of *The Lost Soul of American Politics*, by J. P. Diggins. *New York Review of Books*, February 1985.

Young, Iris Marion. "City Life and Difference." *Justice and the Politics of Difference*. Princeton, N.J.: Princeton University Press, 1990.

INDEX

ABOUT THE AUTHOR

Frank G. Kirkpatrick is Ellsworth Morton Tracy Lecturer and Charles A. Dana Research Professor of Religion at Trinity College in Connecticut, where he has taught since 1969 after earning his PhD from Brown University. Professor Kirkpatrick has written on ethics and in particular on the work on John Macmurray in a variety of articles and books, including *Community: A Trinity of Models* (1986), *Together Bound* (1994), *The Ethics of Community* (2001), and *A Moral Ontology for a Theistic Ethic* (2003). He is also the author of numerous articles in the fields of social ethics and philosophy of religion. He is a member of the American Academy of Religion and the Society for Philosophy of Religion.